God is Not Angry
(the truth that sets us free)

- and -

Your Sins Are Forgiven

by

Ian Petit OSB

New Life Publishing, Luton, UK

This edition published in 2004 by
New Life Publishing
15 Barking Close
Luton, LU4 9HG, UK

God is Not Angry first published in1997
by Darton Longman & Todd and reprinted in 1997 and 1998
Your Sins Are Forgiven first published in 1993
by Darton Longman & Todd and reprinted in 1995 and 1999

ISBN 1 903623 15 4

Cover design by Yvonne Bell, www.vestments.co.uk.
Yvonne creates stoles, chasubles and copes
to individual design, often on silk.

New Life Publishing, Luton UK

Contents

God is Not Angry

Your Sins Are Forgiven

Preface

Fr Ian Petit died shortly after completing this book. We print here the text of the homily given at his funeral by the Abbot of Ampleforth, Patrick Barry OSB.

After Fr Ian's operation we knew how ill he was and how gloomy the doctors' prognosis. Nevertheless the Saints and Angels came to help him and he had a period of remission. During that time we looked together to the future and he said: 'There is only one thing I can do and that is to preach the gospel.' Well, he certainly did know how to preach the gospel; it was his life. And in that preaching he reached into the life of others with healing and inspiration because he relied on the Word of God in the Bible. So today we turn to the Bible in our loss, where we have found the two lessons for our celebration today. They give for our reflection what are perhaps the two key points of Fr Ian's preaching message.

Look at the very first words of the Gospel passage: 'Do not let your hearts be troubled. Believe in God –

believe also in me' (John 14:1). Think how often Ian urged the importance of faith and also of our constant need to be peaceful, confident, untroubled in our faith. Then turning to the first lesson think how typical of Ian's repeated message are St Paul's words to his beloved Philippians: 'Rejoice in the Lord always . . . Let your gentleness be known to everyone. *The Lord is near.* Do not worry about anything, but by prayer . . . with thanksgiving let your requests be known to God. And the peace of God, which surpasses all understanding will guard your hearts and your minds in Christ Jesus' (Philippians 4:4–8). Such was the message from Scripture which Fr Ian has preached all over the world for the last twenty-five years.

That is a wonderful memory and we can cherish it with delight. Even more wonderful, even more powerful is the truth about him that we all know; he always strove to live what he preached – in the gentleness St Paul recommends, in the untroubled faith Christ bequeaths us – while the peace of God which surpasses all understanding did indeed guard his heart and mind in Christ Jesus. We all have serene memories of him; let us cherish them with thanksgiving. But let us remember that his serenity was achieved at a cost. He was a true follower of Christ, so he did not come to the faith, the gentleness, the peace we like to remember without suffering –

without Christ overcoming that suffering through Ian's utter faith in him.

One should be sparing of biography at a funeral, but one cannot grasp the spiritual message of Fr Ian's life without some reference to the road he trod to come to it himself. He first entered this community and gave himself to the Benedictine way of life in 1941. The Benedictine way, which never left him, is radically a way of seeking God. From this – from that seeking pursued in season and out of season – flowed all that was to follow.

He left the monastery with the permission and blessing of Abbot Byrne when his temporary vows ran out four years after joining the community. His search – his seeking of God – continued. There followed four years of lay experience. He started with teaching; that was quite understandable. Then he ventured on what was for him improbable ground. He went into hotel keeping; he actually worked in the Savoy in London. Then – more incomprehensible still for Ian – he worked in an insurance company. After that it is no wonder that he returned to the monastic community here. He pursued his studies for the priesthood. He had a period of study in Paris where he learnt to be fluent in French. Then in 1956 he was ordained priest and this was immediately followed by the Abbot's decision that he must go out as one of the foundation members of St Louis Abbey.

It was a hard, demanding time for all those pioneers. Fr Ian's was a major contribution. He was a brilliant and natural games player and athlete, so he was a gifted coach; but his chief role was as headmaster of the Junior House, where he set the standards and shaped the future with boys of eleven and twelve. None of us here who remember him, especially those who remember him in that role in the Junior House at St Louis, will be surprised that he is still remembered with great affection by men who were boys under his guidance at that time. The lasting devotion of his pupils is testified by Wayne Beugg who is here with us today. He has come on a punishing schedule of great inconvenience to represent others who would like to be here but could not make it. They say that all that time ago Fr Ian had enormous influence on their lives. They recognized him as being close to God. I do not doubt that and I derive from his own account of those years of teaching a further perspective on his success. He says that he knew from his own experience as a boy the agony of not understanding and dreading exposure. So he devoted himself to showing slow students that they could cope. Whatever he says of himself during these years in the St Louis community, he was already a true apostle to the apparently inadequate and a prophet of their bright future. His empathy with and care for the apparently inadequate in the classroom was a foretaste of his empathy in later years with apparent spiritual inadequacy and his faith-filled guidance to Christ's healing.

He has described his breakdown, triggered by strain and overwork, which began a process of profound renewal. It happened in 1968. It was an ominous date, when everything else appeared to be breaking down all over the world. During the following four years or so his search for God was under threat. He took part in and suffered in himself the acute agonies of the time. He never doubted that the outcome could have gone either way; but his faith brought him through, and his gentleness, and his charity, and his personal, though sometimes acutely agonizing openness to personal growth and his readiness to learn from the Spirit working through suffering in his life. He was helped by the prayer of Christians (Catholic and Protestant) in the Charismatic movement especially in America. He found a new openness to ecumenism which enriched his own search for God and later extended his outreach to others in that search.

His search for God changed and developed under the impact of his reading and reflection on the Word of God in Scripture. He came to see God (and everything to do with God) in a different light – the light of love that overcomes fear. The words of St Benedict about how our relationship to God should develop with 'our hearts overflowing with the inexpressible delight of love' became a reality. He entered definitively and unreservedly into the idea of joy in the search for God. At last he had penetrated not the surface words but the deep and lasting reality of the words we have chosen from St Paul for our first lesson today: 'Rejoice in the Lord always; again I will say, rejoice.'

In a recent letter to friends from his sickbed, which he knew was a deathbed, Ian looked back on what he described as: 'his painful journey from the God of fear to the God who forgives and cares.' That journey was a lifelong one but its crisis came at a time when many here and all over the world were falling away. Not only did he not fall away, but in his own renewal discovered anew his mission to preach to others. 'The only thing I know how to do is to preach the gospel.' That is how he summed up the mission he now discovered, in the early seventies. And again he said recently that his mission was not to preach the Charismatic movement but to preach to everyone: 'Salvation through Christ.' In every way and with great generosity he opened out his life to a universal mission in prayer, in preaching, in ecumenism, in outreach (so far as he could) to the whole world.

And the last enemy is death. There is only one who can vanquish that enemy – Christ who is present to each one of us in the Eucharist we offer today. So on his deathbed Ian wrote: 'I hear him say: I came for the weak and when you cannot, I can, whatever touches you touches me and I am the strong one.' Such was the triumphant trust in Christ of the second and last major crisis of his life when he surrendered himself to the final summons of his Lord. How much it was a triumph of grace is proclaimed in the almost Pauline comment which he wrote also from his deathbed: 'I do not intend to sit around waiting to die. While I have life, I want to play my part in helping God's Church become what she should be.' At that time he was, as always, acutely conscious of his weakness, of his dependence, of his vulnerability, and of where and how to find consolation and strength, but he went on serving his Lord, in faith, in prayer, in work.

During this mortal sickness he completed for his publisher his sixth and last book. At the end of that he wrote a reflection which I shall now quote. It reads like a Testament to all of us – a guide to the way he had travelled in his search for God. It may have been the last thing he wrote before Christ called him to share the delight of his risen life in the Father. It is all we need remember of Ian today:

Love is a journey out of self into another. Because of sin, we tend to journey into ourselves. It is only by the power of the cross that we can die to self and truly journey into God. So do not be discouraged at finding prayer difficult. Prayer is not about having heavenly sensations. It is standing in poverty before the One who loves us. It is not easy to stand in poverty; we wish to stand with some success. When all seems dark, it is not necessarily our fault. Perhaps God is purifying us by showing us our poverty. Remember we are ambitious creatures, and we even want to succeed in spiritual things; so be on your guard against wanting to seem to make progress.

'Love is a journey out of self into another.' With that simple but eloquent description of Fr Ian's own journey of faith let us turn to that 'Other', Christ, into whose resurrection Ian's journey is now accomplished. Let us pray for him and for his complete taking up by Christ into the delight of his risen life. Let us pray for all – worldwide – to whom he ministered. And let us imitate his utter faith by which we recognize that the Lord is near. So that by prayer and thanksgiving we may together let our requests be known to God as in the Eucharist Christ offers himself for us and gives himself to us to offer as our own.

PATRICK BARRY OSB
8 November 1996

Introduction

To learn about a God of rules and regulations is to acquire a very distorted picture of God. After all, the way we think about God will determine the way we relate to him. A God who requires our good behaviour will be a God who can instil fear, and this will either make us observant or despairing.

I am afraid that many of us grew up with the idea of a demanding God, and once the wrong picture of God is acquired and is lived with for a long time, it takes a very great amount of effort to remove it. If I am convinced that God is not all that pleased with me, no matter how often I hear Scripture speaking of God's love, I will automatically not apply it to myself. It would have been so much better if we had first met the God who forgives and subsequently learnt about behaviour.

I have met many parents distressed and concerned because their teenage children no longer practise their religion. In my experience so much depends on how the faith was first taught. If the God we were introduced to was a God who required good behaviour, then we got off to a bad start; for we will either have become self-satisfied when we managed to keep the externals, or we will have become anxious and disturbed when we failed.

I grew up before the Second World War when discipline was very much part and parcel of life. At times we may have felt rebellious, but on the whole we buckled down and were none the worse for it. The world today is a very different place and appealing to law and duty does not cut much ice. Therefore trying to make teenagers go to church by appealing to duty will have little effect. Religion has to be more than duty. Unless Christianity has become a life-giving experience for us, and it will be obvious when it has, then what we offer others will have little attraction.

I believe that for many Roman Catholics the Bible has been a closed book and so there has been a serious neglect of God's Word and a serious neglect of one of the main channels by which God communicates with us. The Bible used to be inaccessible to ordinary people either because it was in Latin or in rather archaic English, and even when the translations were good, people still needed educating in how to understand Scripture. It is also true that we were not encouraged to read Scripture. All this meant that a vital way in which God communicates with his people became closed off. To depend just on preaching is a very dicey way to learn about God for if the preacher has been nourished on the God who requires good behaviour, then, while a conscientious lifestyle may be encouraged, an impoverished understanding of the gospel will be imparted.

Not for one moment am I saying that behaviour is not important, but to think that our good behaviour wins us God's approval flatly contradicts the God who came searching for us sinners and paid, at such terrible cost, our debts. What so caught the imagination of the early Christians was the fact that God had come down from heaven, shared their nature, lived among them and made it clear that he was their brother. By his frequent appearances among them after his resurrection, he convinced them that he was still with them, no longer confined to just where his physical body was. Then after Pentecost they all knew, without doubt, that he now indwelt each of them, wishing to share their lives and burdens.

I believe we must refind this God among us, the God who wants to carry our weaknesses, the God who lives in and with us, the brother-God, the God who saves and does not condemn. In order to do this we must take what God has told us, and then conscientiously shape the way we live our lives according to what he has said.

In this book I want briefly to look at some common misconceptions; then to spell out what God has done for us; show how the Church proclaims these truths and give some practical hints on how to shape our lives according to what God wishes. There may be some repetition between chapters, but I leave the text as it is because in my experience we often need to hear things more than once.

At the end of each chapter I have listed various thoughts and suggestions as to how to make that chapter become a living experience. The questions I put could be used in groups, but sensitivity is necessary because the questions need honest answers if they are to be of any use. I fully realize that not everyone will have experienced Christianity in the same way as I have, but, as a priest, I have met enough whose experience has been very similar to mine; for them I write.

⤞ 1 ⤝

Wrong Images of God

*'The lamp of your body is your eye. When your eye is
sound, your whole body too is filled with light; but when
it is diseased your body too will be all darkness. See to it
then that the light inside you is not darkness.'*

(Luke 11:34–5)

Wrong images of God mean a faulty foundation on
which to build, and altering foundations of build-
ings already above ground level is an immense job.
When Jesus told us to remain in his love (John 15:4)
he was not saying something nice that we could
print on posters and feel good about, nor was he
saying something to make our minds search for
interesting insights or thoughts; he was giving us a
command and asking us to obey.

It is fairly easy to remain in God's love when we
feel loved or have accomplished some good work,
for we reason that we are worthy of his love.
However, the time when we must remain in his
love is precisely the time we know we are unworthy
of that love through some sin of ours. Our basic

problem is that we have failed to understand that God's love is not merited. Since we are not able to see or feel God, that means that all our ideas of God will be inadequate, and that is how it has to be; but we must take care that our ideas are not inaccurate. It is all too easy to make God into our own image and likeness, and he then becomes a God of hearsay and not the God of revelation.

I believe it is so difficult to hear God's Word accurately because of the wrong images of God we picked up as we were taught about him. So much depends on how we first heard about God. I appreciate how difficult it is in teaching children not to give the impression that God is looking for their good behaviour. Of course, in one sense this is true, but it is so easy to give the impression that we can decide whether we are good or not. For example, can someone who is greedy stop being greedy by will-power? He may manage not to act greedily, but that does not remove his greedy disposition. Can an impatient person become patient? Clearly she can act as though she were patient, in other words she can hide her impatience but that does not make her a patient person. The same is true of a person driven by sexual desires; he may sincerely not want to be like that, he may never give in to these desires, and he would give much to be rid of them; but is he able to stop having them? The good news of the gospel is about God changing, in our inmost being, those of us who believe in his Son's saving work, thus causing us to behave differently.

The Church is ever in need of reform. No one sets out to teach error, however the father of lies seeks every opportunity to distort the truth and the Holy Spirit is needed to set things right again. Jesus taught about his merciful Father and his constant theme was, 'Blessed are you who need mercy and know it'. Urging people to pull up their spiritual socks and try harder can be commendable, but, if the good news of the gospel has not yet been firmly grasped, this approach can actually encourage precisely what Jesus discouraged, namely self-exaltation.

It is disturbing to see how it was the devout, the conscientious, those who fulfilled meticulously the requirements of the Jewish Law, who were the very ones who seemed most closed to Jesus; on the other hand it was the less observant of the Jewish faith, even the non-believers, who were often the ones most free to hear the Lord's message.

The fact that we get wrong ideas about God must not alarm us. The Apostles had difficulty in trying to understand Jesus. They lived with him and listened to his teaching, but their ideas of him were only formed slowly. What was important was that they kept at it. Idea after idea had to be shattered as they gradually pieced things together. It was only when the Spirit came that they had revelation from within themselves. So, the fact that we misunderstand must not surprise us, but it would be sad if we did not allow the Spirit within us to change our ideas and to change them many times. Wrong ideas result in wrong behaviour, and I want to look now at the sorts of behaviour and attitudes that the wrong fear of God can produce.

Conformity

People react in different ways to excessive fear of God. Any conscientious person will, of course, wish to conform and obey, and this will produce a loyal, observant, regular, dependable type. Such persons can easily be lulled into a false sense of wellbeing, for after all they see themselves as trustworthy and well-behaved. Certainly they have their faults, but they will argue that no one is free of those. What is so tragic about this type of person is that, unknowingly, they prevent themselves from ever meeting the merciful God. After all their virtuous living has cost them much; they are dependable when help is required and so, without ever consciously thinking it, they will feel it is God who owes them something, rather than they who owe God.

In the parable of the two men who went up to the temple to pray, Jesus points out how virtuous people can so easily think of themselves as righteous. It is interesting to note that Jesus pronounces 'justified' he who stood at the back painfully conscious of his sin.

Our observance of the gospel precepts, springing from human nature rather than grace, can block us from hearing God's message of mercy. This blindness stems from our wrong picture of God as the One who needs to be satisfied with our observance. God is not needing to be satisfied, rather he wants us to find our fulfilment in serving him and receiving his love and mercy. In thinking God will be pleased with our serving him, we have things round the wrong way, for he knows we will be fulfilled by serving him because we were made for him and not for ourselves. How much better it would have been if we had first met God as the One who wanted our sins and failures and not our success.

Anxiety

Fear of God can produce conformity or it can make individuals obsessed with their sins and failures. Unlike the first type who saw good in themselves, this type can only see bad. This fills them with anxiety and worry. Every time they come into the presence of God, there is an uneasiness, even an unwillingness to approach him. They imagine his penetrating eyes piercing into them and they are in mortal fear of what he may do to them. They are not wanting to hear his Word for fear they will only hear what is condemnatory. Any words of love or approval, they will apply to other noble souls who have managed to conquer themselves.

Such an attitude clearly shows that it is not the message of salvation in Christ that has penetrated but rather the message of condemnation. The fact that these persons feel unacceptable to God shows that they have not understood that in Christ we are all acceptable. They imagine they are outside Christ and have in some way to merit being in him. Such persons will tend to rely heavily on the prayers of others and will also have an exaggerated devotion towards Saints: trusting in the prayers of these noble souls, they will go from one novena to another and become sitting ducks for any prayer that has attached to it the words 'never found to fail'. ·

It is tragic that the gospel of mercy is thus turned into a gospel of condemnation. All this springs from basic misconceptions picked up in childhood and never corrected. I thank God that today hell-fire sermons and missions of that sort, which carried little of the good news, are no longer with us. But once they certainly were preached, and, alas, there are many still suffering wounds and hurt from them.

Wrong Images of God

It is so hard to get a right balance. God is not an ogre nor is he a benign uncle in the skies. He is a God of mercy, but he can do nothing to save those who wilfully reject him; and to reject the One who gives life brings very serious consequences. Fear of damnation can convert a person, but to live by this fear is to have failed to meet the God of mercy. Again I am more and more convinced that we need ongoing education in the things of God, and it is not a question of simply knowing the truth but of applying it and deliberately living it. 'Remain in my love' is a very definite command.

Resentment

For those of us who remember it, Vatican II challenged the way we thought about God, and it can be very disturbing to discover that what we had been taught was not, apparently, entirely correct. Instead of being relieved to discover that God was a God of mercy and not of condemnation, some people have allowed themselves to feel betrayed and have tried to justify their original ideas; thus they have tended to seize on any text that shows the anger of God, and with a certain satisfaction they say, 'There you are, he is an angry God.' It is threatening to have our understanding of God challenged. The seemingly solid rock on which our faith was once built, suddenly becomes fluid and unstable; and uncertainty often gets expressed as anger.

No idea we have of God can capture him, so we must not become so wedded to our ideas that we never allow them to be changed. This shows again how important it is for us continually to measure our ideas of God against his revelation of himself, and to expect to progress in our understanding.

The Lapsed

There are many who have abandoned God and his Church, but I am convinced that what has actually been abandoned has been a false idea of God and his Church. I know some people who have just abandoned the Church but have not abandoned God. The Church, made up of repenting sinners, can upset and anger people who often react and say they no longer want to have any relationship with an organization that seems so imperfect. Often much time is needed to work through hurts and misunderstandings, but what is sad is that when a person cuts himself or herself off from the Church, that person can be exposed to all sorts of wrong notions and they lack the guidance left them by Jesus in his Church.

Wrong Images of God

My Own Experience

For years I lived with the idea of God watching and recording my every action so he could confront me with all my failures on the Day of Judgement. No one actually taught me that, as far as I can remember, but I certainly picked up the idea that God recorded all our actions, and I know, from counselling others, that I was by no means alone in thinking that. I understood Jesus as a saviour in the sense that he became one of us to teach us what the Father wanted us to do and to give us a demonstration of how to do it. The Gospels are full of injunctions on how we are to behave and Jesus demonstrated his teaching by the way he lived. In other words, he seemed to say that he was a model and we should follow him; 'I am the Way,' he said in John 14.

I certainly admired the teaching, but seemed unable to put it into practice successfully. It was not that I was wicked, but I was certainly not loving, forgiving or patient and I could easily feel guilty every time that I was reminded to love my neighbour. I say all this to show that even though I had a serious misunderstanding as to what Christianity was all about, I was able to live as a practising Christian, going to church, listening to sermons, and yet never having my misunderstanding of the gospel challenged. In retrospect, I suspect the gospel I heard being preached was a gospel of morality.

Jesus' death was for me a tragedy. Here was a good man, the very Son of God, being put to death by sinful humanity who refused to believe who he was. I saw all that as tragic and I could regret it, but I could not see how his death actually affected me. How could an innocent man's death liberate the guilty? I understood the words 'he died for our sins' in the sense he died *because* of our sins, not in the sense of *in order to remove* our sins. Since sin remained with me and I continued to fall into sin, I did not see how Jesus had taken sin away, so naturally I concluded it had yet to happen to me, and it would happen only when I managed to behave myself and do what the Lord had commanded. I had also missed the point of the resurrection: to me this miracle was an outstanding proof that Jesus was the Son of God, therefore we had better take seriously what he taught and behave ourselves. His rising was not for me the beginning of the new human race.

All this goes to show that it is quite possible, while practising as a Christian, to be ignorant of what the gospel is really about. I was baptized, and I firmly believe that was genuine, but I had not been evangelized. I believed that God existed, I believed that Jesus was the Son of God, but I see now that I did not believe in Jesus as my Saviour in the way I now understand it. I listened to numerous sermons but their effect was more moralistic than evangelistic, nice sermons moving me to have spiritual feelings, or rousing me to be more noble and generous, but they were not spelling out loud and clear that Jesus' death had already pardoned me and won new life for me and in him was my hope and salvation.

I am amazed, even ashamed, at the way I saw things. In one sense I was so near the truth that I thought I had the truth. I could be inspired to be the conqueror, to be heroic for the Lord, to smile when broken, to be loving when unjustly treated. The sermons I heard filled me with determination – I would achieve great things for the Lord. The truth was that I was heading for a very necessary fall, and what a fall! I had to see how I was driven by ambition, not the desire to serve; it was pride not love. How difficult it was for me to be told, 'You cannot but I can.' What a long and painful lesson it has been.

Since I never heard the good news of the gospel clearly spelled out, I stumbled along ignorant of my error. I am not blaming those who had charge of me, I am just stating how blind a practising Christian can be, when they do not know the central message: 'cut off from me you can do nothing'

(John 15:5). It makes me wonder how many others there are who are as I was?

Faith Must Be Taught and Lived

I have become more and more convinced that it is in the family where the child learns Christianity. If the parents have false ideas, the chances are the child will learn them also. During the early years of the Church's existence, converts were adults. They heard about Jesus as their Saviour and they wished to be baptized. As time went on parents grew anxious because of the high rate of infant mortality. They were afraid their child might not live to make its own decision for baptism and the Church in her wisdom decided to baptize infants provided the parents brought their child up to understand what he or she had been given. When Christianity had spread over Europe, children grew up in a Christian environment making it easier for them to imbibe Christian standards.

This cannot be said of children growing up today in the western world, where, alas, many families are not strong in their faith, and baptism has often become a thing that one 'ought' to have done. In this sacrament faith is infused into the recipient, but unless it becomes fanned into flame, it can flicker and just fade away or remain dormant. Teaching

Christian doctrine and principles does not necessarily bring to life the dormant faith given at
baptism, for it is not faith in doctrines that gives life,
it is faith in a person.

A person may go regularly to church and practise
their faith without ever coming to a living and life-
giving faith in Jesus Christ and a trust in all that he
has achieved for us. Knowing that he died and rose
again is not the same as trusting in that death and
resurrection. Jesus promised that the Holy Spirit
would remind us of all that Jesus taught and he
would lead us into truth. This surely means leading
us to understand the truth, not just to know it. This
leading is not done by way of argument, that is the
way of reason; rather it is done by allowing our
spirits to be illuminated, so that we know the truth
without necessarily understanding how or why we
know it is true. This is what it means to grasp the
truth spiritually. Such an insight does not usually
come suddenly out of the blue, though of course
God could intervene in this way; normally it comes
as we wrestle with the truth with our intellects,
pondering God's revelation.

When we declare that Jesus is Lord we clearly state
that our salvation does not belong to us through
anything that we have done, we attribute all to the
working of the Lord. That is why no one can say

31

with conviction 'Jesus is Lord' unless they are moved by the Spirit.

All this shows how important sound teaching is and how necessary that it should be ongoing. In the next chapter I will spell out the basic teaching that our faith should rest on. Try to read that chapter listening to the teaching, and not blocking it if you should find it in some way differing from what you think the truth is. Remember we can hang on to that of which we should let go.

For Reflection

Remember it is not easy to communicate ideas of God to someone else. God is Spirit; therefore we must not be surprised when we pick up wrong ideas of God. The point of the following questions is to find out from where our ideas of God have come, if they have changed and if they need further changing. Be honest in your answers. In most cases we will know what the answer should be, but is it our own answer?

- Do you view God with a certain amount of anxiety? Can you say why?
- Can you remember your first thoughts of God – most likely not – but what were your early impressions of him? Have these changed? If so,

what changed them? What do you think God is like now?

- Do you think your ideas have been formed by what God has revealed to you, or from what other people have said? In other words, is your God a God of hearsay or revelation?
- Would you put yourself among those who conform, who try to do what is right? Can you understand how conforming and keeping the rules can shield us from meeting God's mercy?
- Or would you class yourself with the anxious? Can you say why you are anxious? Did Jesus not come for sinners? Why do you feel he did not come for you? Can you see how illogical such an attitude is?
- If you lived through Vatican II, did it please or upset you? Can you say why? Did you feel your ideas of God were threatened? Where did your ideas of God come from?

Right Images

> 'Father, Righteous One, the world has not known you, but I have known you, and these have known that you have sent me. I have made your name known to them and will continue to make it known, so that the love with which you loved me may be in them, and so that I may be in them.' (John 17:25–6)

It is important that wrong images of God are not replaced by more wrong images. The hard-judging God must not be replaced by the benign all-forgiving God who really does not care what we do. We must shape our understanding of God from what God has said about himself and from what plans he has for us. We learn this revelation from the teachings of his Church and from the book of the Church – Scripture.

By the teachings of the Church I mean the universal teachings and not the private opinions of some priest. For example, at the time that I write there is a visionary in Ireland who claims to have visions and messages from God. A number of priests believe the visitations are genuine and they are giving their support to the visionary. This, naturally, adds weight to the visions and messages; but it does not mean the universal Church is giving her support yet. Not everything priests say or teach is necessarily the teaching of the whole Church.

I grew up before Vatican II at a time when priests laid a fairly heavy emphasis on the need to practise the faith, receive the sacraments (particularly confession as it was then called), and I got the impression that failure to comply would result in rather dire consequences. I am not saying that these teachings were false, for if we do reject God and the practice of our faith the consequences are serious, but it is not the intention of the universal Church to give the impression that God is a hard taskmaster; nor is it the intention of the universal Church to teach that God does not really mind what we do.

So How Are We to View the Commandments?

Unfortunately there are many people who see Christianity in terms of learning to be virtuous by overcoming our faults. Yet, surely the briefest familiarity with the gospel shows that Jesus did not come to search out the virtuous, but he came to find and save sinners. How is it we can miss that point? Surely this is the blindness that Jesus so often talks about.

Frequently the gospel is referred to as power:

> I am not ashamed of the Good News: it is the power of God saving all who have faith – Jews first, but Greeks as well – since this is what reveals the justice of God to us: it shows how faith leads to faith, or as scripture says: the upright man finds life through faith.
>
> (Romans 1:16–17)

Left to ourselves we can so easily misunderstand and imagine the power referred to is our own power, and thus we set out on the road to master ourselves. This, alas, only repeats Adam and Eve's fault of imagining that they had the power to direct their own lives. The power of the gospel is in fact precisely opposite – it is surrendering to God's way of doing things. The way God plans to make us holy is for us to depend on what Jesus has achieved through his death and resurrection. In other words, God's way of undoing the Fall is for us to abandon any plan to save ourselves and to depend entirely on what Jesus Christ has done for us. We actually frustrate God's work when we try to win our salvation for ourselves and that is why it is possible to be an observant person but not be holy.

We must not attribute to the Law a power that it has not got. The keeping of the Law makes no one holy, all it does is show that one is holy. When Jesus lives in us and we are submitted to him, then our behaviour is empowered by him and we begin to live in the way that God wishes. But to imagine that the keeping of the Law makes us holy is a vast deception. The Chosen People became observers of the Law, but they missed the Son of God when he came walking down their streets. How blind can one get!

Wrong Emphases

An emphasis on punishment can make God appear rather terrifying, and this has, I believe, blinded many people to the amazing truth of his mercy. Once you have seen God as someone to fear and dread, an immense amount of preaching on his mercy is needed to penetrate that wall of fear. Much healing is needed before the Word of God can penetrate a person whose mind has been paralysed with fear. Clearly any prayers said for healing which are not accompanied by real efforts, on the part of the person prayed for, to stop thinking negatively, will be of little avail. It is necessary for the person prayed for to co-operate with the healing by deliberately breaking the patterns of thought they have fashioned for themselves about God. This is hard work. It is very similar to the exercises that a physiotherapist will set for a patient with damaged muscles. They are often very painful to do, but if neglected, then the cure will not come.

Those seeking healing must fill their mind with true thoughts of God.

> You must give up your old way of life; you must put aside your old self, which gets corrupted by following illusory desires. You must be renewed by a spiritual revolution so that you can put on the new self that has been created in God's way, in the goodness and holiness of truth. (Ephesians 4:22–4)

So if we are to replace wrong ideas about God and his plans for us with the right ideas we need to understand simply and clearly the nature of God's revelation, the meaning of the 'good news'.

The Good News of the Gospel

Clearly there is something amiss with human nature. In the letter to the Romans, St Paul complained that the good he wished to do, he often failed to do; while the evil he wished to avoid, that he did. We have all experienced the same problem. No matter how hard we try, we seem unable to correct our faults. We may manage to hide them, but that does not mean the fault does not persist vigorously in our inner being. Generous actions do not necessarily mean a generous heart. There is a difference between what we are and what we do.

I believe it is so important to understand that it was out of love that the Father sent his Son, and it was also out of love that the Son came. Jesus consented to live in the wounded nature of the sons and daughters of Adam, though we must understand that in him there was no personal sin; he thus made himself one with the human family; and yet with his power as God, he did not live in the way the disobedient children of Adam did, and thus he became the first human being, through his own power, not to dance to Satan's tune.

This, marvellous as it is, would not on its own save the human race; it would only save one member, Jesus Christ himself. But Jesus came to save all of us by removing the blockage of sin between us and God. In order to do this he needed to take the sins of humankind onto himself and pay the penalty himself. Scripture makes a clear statement of this truth: 'For our sake God made the sinless one into sin, so that in him we might become the goodness of God' (2 Corinthians 5:21).

God has revealed to us what went wrong with his creation, what went wrong with human beings. Profound spiritual truths are conveyed to us through the simple story of the garden of Eden. Just as Jesus made up many stories to illustrate his teachings, stories such as the prodigal son and the good Samaritan, so too we find stories in the Old Testament which are not necessarily historical but are used to illustrate a point.

In teaching us about the Fall God uses the story of a garden. In the story Adam and Eve were instructed not to decide things for themselves but to do what God told them; hence the command that they were free to eat from any of the trees in the garden including the tree of life, but they were not even to touch the tree of the knowledge of good and evil. But Adam and Eve ignored the command and the result of the Fall is that their descendants much prefer to live guided by either their feelings or their reason than by what God has said. The tree of life is rejected in favour of the tree of the knowledge of good and evil. Whether the Fall happened exactly in this way is not the most important factor; what is important is that we see its result in us: a rebellious nature. If we are honest, we can see that we much prefer to direct our lives by our feelings and reasoning than by obeying God's Word.

Conscious of the danger of over-simplifying, I will now try to explain in the simplest language I can how God has dealt with the problem.

In order to heal human nature of its wounds from sin, God sent his beloved Son to take on that wounded nature. It would not have been enough for

God to send his Son to take on the nature Adam had before the Fall for that nature was not in need of saving. In some way it was necessary that the Son should assume a fallen nature. But how, we ask, can the sinless One assume a fallen nature?

For years I have wrestled with this question, and I was encouraged to think more about it when I came across the Good News Bible translation of Romans 8:3: 'God condemned sin in human nature by sending his own Son, who came with a nature *like man's sinful nature,* to do away with sin' (my emphasis). It is as though Jesus is saying to us, 'I have not only become one of the human family, I have also allowed myself to become vulnerable like you, to be tempted like you, to experience weakness like you and yet never surrender to these attacks. I have so identified myself with you that your sins have become as though they were mine and I have made reparation for them. 'For our sake God made the sinless one into sin, so that in him we might become the goodness of God' (2 Corinthians 5:21).

Another great help in my thinking came when I was recommended to read *In the Likeness of Sinful Flesh* by Fr Thomas Weinandy OFM Cap. He shows how the Fathers of the Church wrestled with this whole question and indicates that one thing they all seemed to agree on was that if a nature was to be redeemed, then it had to be done from within that nature. St Augustine, for example, said, 'Never would you have been freed from sinful flesh had he not taken on the likeness of sinful flesh' (*Sermons* 185). He also said, 'The Son of God assumed human nature and in it he endured all that belonged to that condition. This is a remedy for mankind of a power beyond our imagining' (*De Agone Christiano* 12).

It must be clearly understood there was no personal sin in Jesus. He took on wounded human nature so that he could live in it but not of it. When we say Jesus took on our fallen nature we mean he took on a nature destined to suffer, die and experience damnation, unless in some way it could be atoned for.

God's rightful judgement on sin is to repel the sinner. This is not a question of God banishing the sinner from himself, but rather the sinner being quite unable to be in God's presence. Jesus did not simply pretend to be incapable of being in God's presence, rather he took our sins on himself at the crucifixion and actually experienced banishment.

Putting it in blunt language, Jesus consented to stand in front of his beloved Father besmirched with our sins and receive from him our sentence. The consequence of sin is more than physical death, it is a wounding that separates us from the Father. The theologian Von Balthasar emphasizes that Jesus stood in the place of sinful humanity and therefore endured the curse of sin. The penalty for sin is, he says, more than physical death, it is the 'second death' and he argues that if Jesus died to pay for all sin he had to endure the complete horror of our sin. 'Jesus does not only accept the mortal destiny of Adam, he also, quite expressly, carries the sin of the human race, and with these sins, the "second death" of God-abandonment' (*Mysterium Paschale* 90).

Because Jesus is God, anything he does will have infinite value; therefore by taking the sins of the world upon himself he could make satisfaction for them by bearing their consequence. So, if Jesus is to atone for every human sin, he has to undergo the punishment for every sin. He, God, bearing as human being all the sins of the human race, could make more than enough satisfaction.

The consequence of even one mortal sin is terrible to contemplate; what the consequence of every human sin would be, does not bear thinking about. I wonder what the words of the creed really mean when they say Jesus 'descended into hell'? The Church, nowadays, observes a great silence from 3.00 p.m. on Good Friday until the beginning of the Easter vigil. No words, ceremonies or actions seem able to cope with the extraordinary lengths God went to save humankind.

The Son of Man must be lifted up
as Moses lifted up the serpent in the desert,
so that everyone who believes may have eternal
  life in him.
Yes, God loved the world so much
that he gave his only Son,
so that everyone who believes in him may not
  be lost
but may have eternal life. (John 3:14–16)

Because the consequence of all sin has been met, all sins, even future sins, have been paid for. This does not mean that all sinners have been pardoned, but it does mean forgiveness is available for all sinners who repent, confess and wish to reform.

Also, when Jesus died, his Adam nature was put to death. On rising from the dead, he did not come back to life in the same way that Lazarus did, he rose to be the new Man. From him would come the new human family, restored to the favour of the Father.

So two mighty happenings occurred on Calvary. Firstly all sins were paid for; secondly the Adam nature was put to death, thus making way for the new Adam to rise from the dead and begin the new race of humans for God. This is the good news of the gospel and this is the message that the universal Church teaches.

<u>For Reflection</u>
- As you read this chapter, did you have any new insights, or a deeper appreciation in your understanding of the mystery of redemption?
- How much of a human being do you think that Jesus became? Do you think that he would have known everything? Do you think his answers to tricky questions came because he was God or do you think these came from the Holy Spirit who was guiding him? Read Matthew 12:25–8.
- If Jesus, who is God, paid for our sins, that means your sins have been paid for. How much does this fact comfort you, or does it perhaps not comfort you? If not, could it be that you do not believe it because you do not feel it?
- Have you understood that it is the death and resurrection of Jesus that has saved you and not the observance of the Law?
- Remember what is important is not that you just gain new knowledge, but that you use that knowledge to shape the way you live your life.

∞ 3 ∞

The Church Proclaims This Truth

And let me warn you that if anyone preaches a version of the Good News different from the one we have already preached to you, . . . he is to be condemned.

(Galatians 1:8)

St Paul was absolutely astonished that the Galatians had so promptly turned away from the gospel and had 'decided to follow a different version of the Good News' (Galatians 1:6). 'Does God give you the Spirit so freely and work miracles among you because you practise the Law, or because you believed what was preached to you?' (Galatians 3:5) Here Paul is asking us the pertinent question: 'Is it by faith in what Jesus has done that we receive salvation, or is it by our observance?'

It is the duty of the Church to proclaim from one generation to the next what God has accomplished through the death and resurrection of his Son. She does this in her liturgies, her sacraments, her prayers and her teaching. St Paul condemns anyone who fails to do this. The question we need to ask ourselves is, do we hear the Church proclaiming this message? Of course, if we do not know this wonderful message we can easily miss hearing it when it is proclaimed; but if we do know it, is our experience of church a place where we are reminded constantly of the good news and are encouraged to believe and have hope?

The Church spends the whole year highlighting various aspects of the salvation story, so that her members hearing it will give thanks to God, and through their acts of faith will experience the power of salvation. It is interesting to note how often Jesus told those who had been healed: 'It is your faith that has saved you.' St Paul described the good news as 'the power of God saving all who have faith' (Romans 1:16). So in calling to mind the events by which God has saved us, the Church wants us to experience the power of those events as we allow them to be presented to us.

Signs and Words

The Church uses ceremonies and words to remind us of those saving events. These ceremonies are not just theatre for as people witness them, calling the great events to mind with a living faith, the past is able to affect us in the present.

So how important it is that those attending Mass

should be firmly rooted in their understanding of the gospel and its saving power. Where that understanding and appreciation are missing, liturgies and ceremonies will be judged from a merely human point of view. Some people will like one form of ceremony, others will prefer another. Good taste will often clash with more popular tastes, and the very thing that should unite people becomes a painful source of division. What makes a service good is not whether we like it or enjoy it, but whether it clearly celebrates the saving work of the Lord.

Sacraments Proclaim This Truth

After Vatican II the Church revised the rites of sacraments so as to help the faithful appreciate what the sacrament was signifying and accomplishing in the recipient. As in all ceremonies it is the duty of the minister to explain what those attending are about to witness so that they can fully participate.

Baptism

Through baptism something very great, which has already happened, becomes real in the recipient. We are taught that in this sacrament we die with Christ and rise again to new life with him. But I wonder how much of a reality that is for us? It is not that we are 'to feel dead and risen', rather we are to accept that 'we *have* died and *have* risen with him'. All this has happened in the realm of the spirit, and not yet in the realm of our body; that is why it does not touch our senses. Faith calls us to believe, and it is the believing that makes what Jesus has done affect us. 'Your faith has saved you' (Luke 7:50).

Jesus has paid for all our sins, he has reconciled us with the Father, making us children of the Father by uniting us to himself. This means we can stand reconciled before the Father and, even if serious sin should crop up, we have a way back to the Father by invoking what Jesus has done for us. Sacraments are God's way of making happen, throughout the centuries, what his Son achieved in his lifetime here on earth and through his death and resurrection.

Because of what Jesus has done, made real to us through our baptism, we live in the One who has reconciled us to the Father. In him we are safe. If we do not believe that he has reconciled us to the Father and do not live in that truth, we will draw no comfort from the doctrine of the resurrection. If we really believe that we have eternal life, that we are loved by the Father, and that we live in his Son, then surely none of the cares of this life should overshadow those truths.

In celebrating a baptism the Church recalls by signs and words the truth that Jesus laid down his

Adam life in death and on rising he did not take up again that wounded life: he became the new Adam. Going down under the water signifies descending with the Lord into the tomb, and coming up out of the water signifies rising with him to a new life. It literally is being born again of water and the Holy Spirit. Today we do not dunk babies, instead water is poured over their head, but this sign is not as good as it gives the impression of a washing rather than a dying. It is interesting that full immersion baptisms are now beginning to happen again in the Catholic Church.

The new life we receive at our baptism does not mean that we are taken over by some new force and are therefore completely changed. Just as with our birth in the natural order we are responsible for developing the life we received, so too with our birth at baptism we have responsibility to develop what we have been given. When we were born, potentially we had the power to walk, talk, tie our shoes, but it was we who had the life, not the life which had us. So too with this new life received at baptism – we have to learn how to use it. 'I am the vine, you are the branches,' says Jesus (John 15:5). We are united to the Risen One and we have to learn how to draw powerful life from him. Only by listening to his Word, and hearing him tell us 'be brave, I have conquered' (John 16:33) do we come to a trust that believes in what he says. It is this believing that releases in us his power.

Eucharist

In this sacrament the central teaching of the Church is proclaimed again in several very short phrases in the Eucharistic prayers. The beginning of Eucharistic prayer number three, for example, sums up in a very brief way the essence of the gospel: 'All life, all holiness comes from you through your Son, Jesus Christ, by the working of the Holy Spirit'. Holiness, salvation, is not something we achieve by our good works. It comes from the Father who sent his Son to become the holy Man and it is the Holy Spirit who communicates that holiness to us.

All the Eucharistic prayers proclaim this truth of salvation coming through the death and resurrection of Jesus. In calling it to mind, we are made present to Calvary. This does not mean that we repeat what is unrepeatable; rather it means that Calvary is made present to us, is re-presented to us. Hearing the words and seeing the signs we bow in faith before the reality that has saved us, and we acknowledge Jesus to be the Lord and Saviour. Thus we demonstrate our faith in what Jesus has done for us and cause his salvation to flood into us. Clearly if we are wilfully not present, save in body, the effect of what is happening is diminished for us.

In taking communion and consuming the elements we show our acceptance of what has been done for us by willingly identifying ourselves with the body and blood of Christ.

Reconciliation

Confession, as it used to be called, was perhaps the sacrament most in need of revision. It is now called the sacrament of reconciliation and I personally think it still has a long way to go. In the past many people were loyal and frequented this sacrament regularly, but they did not always have an experience which was uplifting. Some confessions, alas, were more like a tribunal than a healing, with the result that God's mercy was obscured. So, when the Church suggested that confessions might be fewer in number but more honest in content, many people dropped the habit of going. I propose now to spend a little time on this sacrament, looking at the meaning of such phrases as 'taking sin away', and considering the place of penance, and our reasons for doing it.

In the sacrament of reconciliation, when the priest absolves the penitent, the Calvary message is proclaimed. When the priest gives the absolution he says: 'God, the Father of mercies, through the death and resurrection of his Son, has reconciled the world to himself and sent his Holy Spirit among us for the forgiveness of sins.' There again is the statement of truth – it is through the death and resurrection of Jesus Christ that all sin has been forgiven and through the work of the Holy Spirit that sinners are reconciled to the Father.

On Calvary Jesus dealt with all sins, even sins that had not yet been committed. This does not mean that all sinners, after Calvary, are automatically pardoned; it means that any *repenting* sinners after Calvary can have the work of Calvary applied to them. At baptism all the sins of the person being baptized are wiped out. But, as we all know, sin can still be committed after baptism. However, God in his mercy has made provision for this in the sacrament of reconciliation. It is important to remember that sacraments are not magic. We need to exercise our faith in the atoning work of Calvary and receive forgiveness through the medium of this sacrament. So when we confess our sins to God we are really only claiming the pardon that was obtained for us at terrible cost long, long ago. All sins committed after baptism can be exposed to the redeeming work of Jesus.

John the Baptist pointed Jesus out as 'the lamb of God that takes away the sin of the world' (John

1:29). But for much of my life my experience of confession was that my sin did not seem to be taken away and so I feared this was another proof that I was unsaved. Jesus came to take sin away, but I continued to sin, so clearly his redemption had not affected me. The concept of 'taking away sin' can be understood in different ways. Sins separate a person from God, and the death of Jesus can take that separation away. Jesus alone has made reparation for us, and the only thing we can do to reverse the situation is to call on that reparation obtained by the death of the Lord. In that sense sins (or the blockages caused by sin) are taken away. It is not enough to know this truth, we must trust in it and act upon it. To act upon it means to confess our sins to God and then know that our sins have been removed. It is not a question of feeling that they have been removed, it is a question of faith. The teaching of the Church is that all sins have been pardoned through the death of Jesus, so whenever a sin is confessed with true regret, then what Jesus did on Calvary is made effective in the sinner. The question we need to ask ourselves is, 'Do I really believe that when I acknowledge my sin to God, Jesus declares me "not guilty any more because he has dealt with it"?' Many of us still walk around carrying the weight of past sin.

Another way of understanding what 'taking away sin' may mean is to rephrase it as 'we stop sinning'.

Part of God's plan is for us to stop sinning: Jesus did not come just to obtain pardon for our sins, he also came to take them out of our lives. By his death, Jesus put the old Adam life to death and paid the penalty for our sins; by his rising to new life, he has made it possible for us to have this new nature, a nature by which we no longer need to sin.

This does not mean that at baptism Jesus comes within us to live our lives for us; he comes rather to live with and in us so that we are able to draw on him for new life and power and when tempted we can share his strength to fight successfully. New life is given us in our spirit and our mission in life is to allow this new, powerful life to come into its own. As I have said, it is not as though our life was being lived for us. It is still our life, but we can choose continually to draw on the life of Christ in us, so that with him we begin to be changed more and more into his likeness.

Penance

An obvious question arises here over the fact that we are often given a penance to perform after we have been reconciled. If Jesus has paid for our sins, we may ask, what is the place of penance? Why are we often given a penance in the sacrament of re-conciliation? And what about places like Lough Derg in Ireland, and the role that penance has played in the history of the Catholic Church?

In the early history of the Church when sins were confessed, a public penance was imposed which was performed communally in Holy Week, and then absolution was given. The performance of the penance reflected the interior disposition, and the giving of a penance after confession today has the same motivation. We are asked to do something to demonstrate our sorrow. But we must remember that it is not the performing of the penance that absolves us, but the absolution. The acts of penance are outward signs of inward regret.

But such acts can also be ways of making reparation for our sins because sin is not just against God: it affects ourselves and it affects others. Say, for example, that I teach someone how to shoplift; I am responsible for teaching another to do wrong. I may lose contact with that person but he or she may well now have started out on a life of sin. I can confess my sin to God and receive forgiveness, but that does not deliver the person I taught to sin. As a member of the Body of Christ I can ask Jesus to breathe his Spirit into that part of his Body which I have so deeply wounded. Just as the human body works for the good of each part, so the mystical Body can, through the power of Jesus, affect each member. It is one thing to say sorry, it is another to show by some sacrifice that I am truly sorry. Through the sacrament of reconciliation our relationship with God is repaired, but the harm done to ourselves and others is not repaired; and this is where acts of penance come in. It is the way by which we try to deal with the harm we have done, and what we do not pay off in this life we pay for in purgatory.

Knowing that all our sins, even the ones not yet committed, have been dealt with, should inspire us with confidence that God in his love has made provision for our future, he has a remedy for our foolish ways. This, of course, does not give any of us the liberty to sin knowing that forgiveness is readily available, for unless there is a sincere desire to reform accompanying our confession the sacrament is not effective.

A conscientious person can quite often still feel guilty even after the sacrament of reconciliation, and I believe this means they are putting more trust in their feelings than in what God has done and what the Church teaches. A person with a conscience that has been dulled may commit the same sin as the conscientious person and yet feel no guilt. At one extreme there are those whose consciences are almost dead and at the other those whose consciences are oversensitive. Guilt is a matter of fact, not feeling. Feelings may accompany sin or they may not. Living by faith requires discipline and courage.

Confirmation

Twice in the life of Jesus the Holy Spirit acted very decisively. The first of these instances was at the incarnation when the Spirit of God overshadowed Mary and the Word became flesh. How fitting it is that as we begin our new life in Christ it is through the working of the same Holy Spirit that this new life comes about. The second time that the Spirit acted very powerfully in the life of Jesus was at the Jordan when the Spirit came down on the Son, empowering him for his public life and for his encounters with the evil spirit. We, too, need to be filled with the same powerful Spirit and his gifts as we begin our adult lives as Christians.

At confirmation the Holy Spirit gives us two sets of gifts: one is for our own personal growth, which of course will ultimately profit the whole Body of Christ; the other set, called charismatic gifts, is given for the building of the Body, the Church.

The Sacrament of the Sick

Jesus never treated sickness as something that came from God. He healed many sick people and told his Church to preach the good news and heal the sick, for while the victory has already been won by Jesus Christ it has still to be worked out in a world that has its course to run. By healing bodies Jesus showed he had power over the devil. Bodily health, though, is not as important as spiritual health, and while there is a sacrament for the sick which is concerned with healing, we still have to face the mystery of suffering and how God can triumph over misfortune without actually removing it. This is a vast subject and I do not intend to cover it here.

Orders and Marriage

Two walks in life which need special empowering are priesthood and marriage. What is important about these sacraments is that they endure and we are meant to call on their power when times get rough.

The priest has two functions whereby he acts above his natural powers and for these acts he too needs God's power: when he consecrates the bread and wine, and when he absolves sins. By a special sacrament he is united to the risen Christ to perform these two functions. He is also ordained to preach the Word of God and to guide and encourage the flock.

With regards to marriage we live in a world that idolizes romantic love and I believe this can play havoc with people brought up in our contemporary 'me-generation'. From all sides we are urged to enjoy, to get the best out of, to spoil ourselves — in other words the emphasis is on what we *get*, not what we *give*. But feelings are rather like the English weather, you cannot rely on them. If two people enter marriage hoping for what they will get out of it, then it is doomed to failure. Rather, we should enter this state seeing what we can give to the other. God plans to make two out of the one; and the world needs to see more of such unions. To be able to live like this day in and day out, requires more than just what human nature can give. In the sacrament of marriage Christ promises to be in each partner, helping and empowering, so that a stable relationship can develop where children may be brought up safely. I believe it is so important that the ongoing nature of these two sacraments be grasped and called upon in times of stress and discouragement.

All a sacrament is doing is calling to mind some aspect of the salvation Jesus won for us and saying: 'We now make this happen to you.' By these sacred signs we are nourished, healed, forgiven, strengthened and empowered. Again, what Jesus has done is vividly called to mind, not just in words and signs, but in effective action.

Scripture

Another great way that the Church should proclaim the good news is through expounding Scripture.

Scripture combines what God has revealed in the Old Testament with the new teaching he gave when he came among us. The new teaching was preached orally to start with and began to be written down from around the year 50 AD onwards.

Scripture is the Word of God and it must be treated and seen as the very Word of God. Through his Word God speaks to his people, so the Church must ensure that the people hear his Word. She uses this Word during her times of worship; and during the Eucharist, where Word and sacrament are celebrated together.

Alas, many of us were not brought up with a strong emphasis on Scripture, and I believe we need to find ways of helping people to learn to love the Word of God. It is not a book we can just pick up and fall in love with. We need help. Let me give a few hints.

Today education tends towards the more practical aspects of life. We want to know how everything works, we want to understand, we want to be masters. We are rapidly losing the need for 'mystery' in our lives and with this we lose the ability to reverence what we cannot explain. So, when God does deign to speak to us we want to be able to understand and agree with all he is saying. In other words, we tend to use our reason to judge God's ways of doing things. When we do not understand his ways, we tend to reject him. In doing this we just repeat what happened at the Fall.

In the Old Testament God chose a nation to become his own people and he tried to get them to trust in his way of doing things. Often his ways were very contrary to their human ways. God was trying to undo the Fall by having a people who would trust in him and not in themselves. The founder of this race was Abraham, and look what a man of faith he was. Alas his descendants were unable to follow his example. Finally God declared that he was going to re-make the human family from the inside; he promised them a new heart and a new spirit. Jesus is of course the one with the new heart and new spirit. But as we read the strange stories in the Old Testament it helps us if we realize that we are not just reading interesting stories, there is a reason behind all that is happening. Yet, if we do not know the message God is trying to teach his Chosen People, then we too will be bewildered by these stories.

If our understanding of the gospel has been shaped by constantly hearing of our need to conform and behave, with a threat of trouble if we do not, then such passages, stating that salvation is a gift, will not make much sense and they will cut no ice. One could argue that such passages should challenge these attitudes, and indeed they should;

but when attitudes have been formed over many years, and when the voice of Scripture has been all but silent, they simply do not have much effect.

The Bible is not just a liturgical book only to be used in church; it is God's love letter to us and should be read and treasured by all of us in the quiet of our homes. It is the work of the Church to open this book to its members, to enable them to read for themselves the mighty things God has done for them. Today, twenty-five years after the Second Vatican Council, I know many Catholics who still do not read Scripture for themselves. It is not for want of trying, but unless they have been fired up with what God has done, they will see much of the book as just rules and regulations with either a reward or punishment awaiting them at the end.

The point I want to make is that if we, Catholics, did not hear the good news preached from the pulpit, we certainly did not receive it from Scripture because few of us read Scripture on our own. The result is that many today are ignorant of the good news. Even when the good news is preached or salvation passages are read from Scripture, the message simply does not penetrate because a mind-set blocks out the truth. On the retreats and missions that I lead, I discover where people are in their walk with God, and many good loyal souls are painfully ignorant of the real meaning of the gospel. I do not condemn these good people, for I, even after ordination, thought salvation was something I achieved by being faithful to the practices of the Church. I had good teachers, but I heard everything through ears that had picked up the message 'God wants you to behave well and you are for the high jump if you don't do it.'

The message of salvation in Christ needs to be proclaimed and proclaimed again and again. I rather imagine we tend to think that if people are baptized, then they have been evangelized. Even though I now know the good news, I have continually to remind myself of it, for it can easily be carried out of my mind by the great deceiver; remember, for example, that the seeds falling on the path were eaten up by the birds (Matthew 13:5). It is for this very reason that the Church keeps bringing before us the message of the gospel in its liturgical celebrations, and putting responses on our lips which affirm that we do believe.

For Reflection

Remember the object of these reflections is to check that our thinking is in line with what God has revealed. It is not a question of how clever we are, so we must not be upset if we find we are often wrong in the way we have understood. After all that is a step forward.

- How would you explain what you understand by 'sacrament'? Slightly magical? Or do you really see the sacraments as Christ's redeeming work being made effective in you?
- Do you look on your baptism as a 'passed event', or do you daily accept it as a reality?
- Do you experience the Church as the 'proclaimer' of the good news or is it an organizer?
- How do you judge liturgy? By your likes or dislikes? Or do you judge it more by whether or not it fans into flame your faith?
- Is the Bible a living book for you? Read the following passages and ask yourself if we dare to believe what they say:

God chose us to possess salvation through our Lord Jesus Christ, who died for us in order we might live together with him, whether we are alive or dead when he comes.

(1 Thessalonians 5:9–10)

It is by grace that you have been saved through faith; not by anything of your own, but by a gift from God; not by anything you have done, so that nobody can claim the credit. (Ephesians 2:8–9)

All I want to know is Christ and the power of his resurrection. (Philippians 3:10)

Can we honestly read these and still think that salvation is our work?

- The liturgy proclaims the same message: 'All life, all holiness, comes from you [Father] through your Son, Jesus Christ our Lord, by the working of the Holy Spirit' (Eucharist, prayer number 3). Where in that passage do we hear that holiness is our work?

- The prayer said at the end of the rosary repeats the same message: 'O God, through the life, death and resurrection of your Son, you have purchased for us the rewards of eternal life . . .' Who has won eternal life for us?

- Do you see the Church as a clerical organization with lay people playing a minor part? Is it 'them and us'?

- Do you regard yourself as part of the Church or would you consider yourself to be on your own?

- Do you see the Church as Christ continuing his work of salvation on earth?

- Do you consider Church members as members of the Body of Christ? We all know the right answer, but how do you actually see them?

⨳ 4 ⨳

Keep Us Faithful to Your Teaching

Lord Jesus Christ, Son of the living God, by the will of
the Father and the work of the Holy Spirit, your death
brought life to this world. By your holy Body and Blood
free me from all my sins and from every evil. Keep me
faithful to your teaching, and never let me be parted
from you.

(Prayer said just before communion)

If we are to remain faithful to Jesus' teaching, then
we must learn what it means to live by faith. Faith is
not a question of assenting to a series of doctrines,
rather faith is expressed by the way we live. If God
tells us that he is with us and on our side, then the
way we live our lives should show that.

If we won the national lottery we would not
profit from it if we never knew that we had won.
Just imagine having this vast prize and not knowing
about it! Once we did learn the truth, then we
would have to make our claim and show we were
the lawful winners; in other words we would have
actively to receive the prize. However, there is the

danger that the prize could go to our heads and it could bring ruin and disaster into our lives. If we were really to profit from it we would need to learn to use it wisely.

Jesus has won for us something far greater than the national lottery; he has won for us reconciliation with the Father and a new life. If we are to profit from this we must claim what he has done for us and then consistently use it wisely.

What Jesus has won for us is in the spiritual plane, and because we neither see it nor feel it, we need consistently to receive it by faith. Satan's work is to accuse the brethren. We are all conscious of our past sins and these can make us feel guilty, unworthy, even condemned before God. The truth is that Jesus has taken all our sins onto himself, and as we confess our sins to God, Jesus declares that we are 'not guilty' because he has dealt with them, and he confirms that we are now in good relationship with God. Living in the knowledge and assurance of this truth is what I mean by living by faith.

What a terrible misunderstanding it would be, not to know a great prize had been won for us and to imagine it was up to us to earn it! But this is exactly how many of us perceive salvation − we believe that it is up to us − and we can perhaps now see the immense harm wrong images about God can do. The harm is by no means easily removed; it has become ingrained into our very being and affects all that we do and think. It is a slow, lengthy process to shake ourselves free of such patterns of thought, but with persistent efforts to replace wrong images with right ones, we can find liberty. Unfortunately, many of us have not met the God who has won so much for us, rather we seem to have met a God who requires us to win by our own efforts.

In this chapter, I want to look at faith and how we can live it in our lives. God's way of saving is through faith. The Fall came about through lack of faith and trust in God, through disobedience. Adam and Eve were told not even to touch the tree of the knowledge of good and evil. By picking its fruit they showed they did not believe what God had said and so they disobeyed his command.

It seems right and fitting that the consequences of the Fall should be reversed by the human family trusting and obeying the Lord no matter what he asked. But where could such a person be found, since all born from Adam and Eve were wounded? God, in his love and mercy, provided that person by sending his beloved Son to come in flesh and obey and trust his Father even in the most dire conditions. This act of obedience reconciled the human family with God. All those who wish to profit from this work of the Son are asked to go the way of obedience and trust; as they put their trust in what Jesus has done for them God promises he will justify and save them.

Even from the earliest days of his dealings with humankind God made it clear that he would act when men and women believed and trusted completely in him. Paul, writing to the Galatians, showed how it was faith, and not observance, that made God fulfil his promise to Abraham: 'Take Abraham, for example: he put his faith in God, and this faith was considered as justifying him' (3:6).

The Constant Temptation

With the introduction of the Law a good number of years later it was all too easy to misunderstand and to imagine that keeping the Law would merit a reward. However, all the Law is capable of doing is showing up our weakness through our inability to keep it. We must not attribute to the Law powers it does not possess by imagining that, if we keep it, it will make us holy. The Law has no power to make holy, no power to change the human heart: all it can do is show up the sinfulness of the human heart. For after all, it is possible to observe the Law externally while the heart is corrupt. The only way the human heart is changed is through the death and resurrection of Jesus Christ, God made man. As I have pointed out earlier there is a difference between being patient and acting as though we were patient. Law-keeping shows there is holiness, it does not produce it.

The constant temptation is to turn God's desire to save us into a religion. Religion comes from the word *ligare* meaning 'to bind'. Thus humans tend to bind themselves to a deity for protection and blessings. I suppose most of us start our journey towards God with this idea in mind, thinking that if we do what pleases God then he will bless and reward. Hopefully we soon learn that it is not a matter of earning brownie points but rather of learning how graciously to accept grace. The commandments, if kept, are not meant to be rules winning rewards, they are rather guidelines as to how God would have us behave.

The one re-occurring sin of the Chosen People was apostasy or lack of trust in God. Constantly they were tempted to rely on observance of the Law rather than the Lord. In the early days of the Church it was very difficult for the new converts not to feel guilty when they did not observe the Law of Moses. As I have said earlier, St Paul forcefully argues that Abraham was saved by faith, not by observance of the Law, showing that God's plan has always been to save humans by faith. It is so hard for us to receive, we much prefer to achieve (see Romans 3:21; 4:9; 4:13).

We do not need to read very far into the Gospels before picking up how much Jesus valued faith. He was literally astonished when the Roman Centurion talked about being unworthy to have him, the Lord, enter his house and then stated that all that was needed was for Jesus to say the word and his will would be done. Jesus exclaimed that he had not met such faith anywhere in Israel (Matthew 8:10). At another time he stressed the need for faith in prayer, 'believe you have it already, and it will be yours' (Mark 11:24). To the woman who touched his garments he said, 'Courage, my daughter, your faith has restored you to health' (Matthew 9:22), and to the one who washed his feet with her tears he said, 'Your faith has saved you' (Luke 7:50).

These accounts are not just given as stories to edify us, they are given for our teaching. Eve chose not to live by God's word, but rather to live by what attracted her senses and appealed to her reason. The fruit of the tree 'was good to eat and pleasing to the eye, and . . . desirable for the knowledge it could give' (Genesis 3:6). God reverses that order when he asks us to live by faith. We are called to trust in what God has said or done and this can appear unattractive, even unwise. St Paul tells us that God chose to save us 'through the foolishness of the message' (1 Corinthians 1:21). All this is not easy for us in our fallen nature, but where faith in Jesus is lacking, then the power of Jesus is blocked. Could this, I wonder, account for the drabness of the lives of many Christians? It is not that God does not want us to be good and do good; not for a moment am I saying such a thing. But, salvation comes through what Jesus has done, not by anything we do.

I know it sounds simple to say that it is through faith in Jesus that we are saved, but to live by faith is actually very costly. Grace is not cheap, it demands that constantly we choose to rely on another and not on self, to rely on another's achievements and not on our own. That does not come easily to us.

Living by Faith

Before we can live by faith we have to have a very clear insight into what to believe. That is why sound teaching is so necessary. How important it is that anyone learning about faith should meet the loving God, full of love and compassion, who, while not benign and uncaring about sin, is always ready to forgive and pardon those who repent.

Unfortunately not all of us have met this loving God, and hellfire sermons of judgement and condemnation have left their all but indelible mark on our lives. Systematic prayer and discipline in replacing false images of God with the truth can do

73

wonders to set people free; as we read in John's Gospel, 'and the truth will make you free' (8:32).

If we want to experience this liberation we must determine to set out on the hard road of faith. St Benedict told his monks that the necessary strictness of discipline might appear daunting at the beginning of their monastic life, but the would-be-monk must not 'be dismayed and run away from the way of salvation, of which the entrance must needs be narrow. But as we progress in our monastic life and faith, our hearts will be enlarged and we shall run with unspeakable sweetness of love in the way of God's commandments' (Rule of St Benedict: Prologue).

Faith involves more than believing that God exists or that he is the Creator. Believing there is a God, or believing that God became man is not the same as believing in God or in his Son. Believing that God exists, but not allowing that knowledge to influence our lifestyle in any way can hardly be called a life-giving faith. Faith is more than assenting to doctrines, it is putting our hope and trust in a Person. Nor is it a one-time act: it is a continuing act; rather like singing a song you have to do more than just get started.

St Paul tells us: '. . . guided by the Spirit you will be in no danger of yielding to self-indulgence . . . led by the Spirit no law can touch you' (Galatians

5:16–18). Most of us tend to live our lives directed by what we feel or think. Jesus taught that we must live by 'every word that comes from the mouth of God' (Matthew 4:4). He told us that his words 'are spirit and . . . life' (John 6:63). To live in the spirit does not mean to live an airy-fairy life being constantly nudged by the Spirit; it means deliberately taking what God has said and applying it to the way we live our lives. A spiritual person is one who lives by what God has said and not by feelings or reasoning alone, which is what is meant by 'living in the flesh'.

Feelings are not wrong, they just happen to be very unreliable. Who, for example, can account for the moods that suddenly drift over us? What once seemed so full of hope can suddenly become unattractive and forbidding. Reason, too, is one of God's great gifts to us, but it is limited; with regard to spiritual truths human logic is of little help. If we are going to be people of the spirit we need to read systematically of God's revelation, we need to listen to him in prayer and obey him.

Faith is not something that concerns the intellect alone, it has to show itself in action. St James stresses that faith must be seen (2:18). Both faith and works are necessary and it is sad when one aspect is stressed to the detriment of the other. It is not enough to know what Jesus has done for us if we do not let that truth affect the way we live our lives. Faith is not a question of rejoicing that we are glory bound; faith changes the way we live on earth because we are glory bound.

To live by faith means making a very deliberate act to shape our way of living by the truth. If the Son of God took my sins onto himself and paid the debt, once I have confessed, I must deliberately believe I am reconciled to God. It does not matter what my feelings happen to be at that moment.

A God of Revelation or Hearsay?

Once we have lost sight of Jesus as the One who came for sinners and see him as the One who came to teach us how to live rightly, then we have lost sight of the good news and have stood the gospel on its head. Jesus did not come to teach us how to strive for perfection and thus merit heaven; he came to hold up the mirror of perfection so that we, seeing our imperfections, would turn to him and would allow him to heal us. We can become so preoccupied with being virtuous that we either become discouraged with our failures, or blinded with our imagined virtues. So we need to ask ourselves just who is the God we are serving? Is he the God of revelation or of hearsay? When the God of revelation is no longer our nourishment, we can fall quickly into devotions. We become prey to saying numerous prayers, especially to this or that saint; to numerous acts of penance as though the salvation of the world depended on us; to this prayer followed by that prayer until the list is endless and it all becomes a marathon and a chore.

We Have No Excuse

Look at the Gospels and see how Jesus sought out sinners. Jesus is the same today as he was then: he seeks out sinners. But do our failures keep us from him? If so, then we have a clear example of how our false ideas of God keep us away from the real God. Our sins should certainly distress us, but they should not discourage us and keep us from the God who is such a mighty champion on our side. God has done the great work of our salvation; our task is to believe it has been done and to accept that the Holy Spirit is accomplishing it in us by encouraging us to believe (faith) and receive (sacraments). 'By virtue of that one single offering, he [Jesus] has achieved the eternal perfection of all whom he is sanctifying' (Hebrews 10:14,15). This quote from Hebrews talks about something that has been achieved and yet it also speaks of a sanctification that is ongoing. This sums up so clearly that the work of Jesus is finished, there is nothing more for him to do, but the work is not yet complete in us. This is the work of the Holy Spirit. We need to nourish ourselves on these truths.

Fundamentalism

But, we can say, is there not a danger of falling into fundamentalism if we simply obey God's Word? We need to remember that God's Word comes to us through the Church and through the Book of the Church – the Bible – and that God did not make us pure spirit, he gave us a body and a mind. Because of the Fall we tend to listen more to our body or our mind than to our spirit, with the result that we have developed our body and our mind and have neglected our spirit. Our bodies are to cope with the physical world, our minds with the intellectual world and our spirits with the spirit world. When we talk about living in the world of the spirit we do not mean we are to ignore our body and become all spirit. For example, when the Bible says, 'Pluck your eye out' (Matthew 5:29), my reason tells me that is not wise. After all the Bible also makes it very clear that Jesus always showed mercy towards sinners, so my reason tells me it would be foolish to condemn the body even though its members may lead me into sin. God also speaks through his Body, the Church, and when I am not clear what his Scriptures are saying, I can ask the Body and be protected from the wiles of the Evil One. So our body and mind are important; living in the spirit does not mean neglecting them, but rather means keeping a proper balance.

Spirit

Whenever Scripture refers to the word 'spirit' we need to note if it refers to our spirit or the Holy Spirit. Whenever a capital 'S' is used, the spirit referred to is the Holy Spirit, when a small 's' is used then it means our spirit or an evil spirit. For example: 'The Spirit himself and our spirit bear united witness that we are children of God' (Romans 8:16).

St Paul is always urging us to live in the spirit and not in the flesh. To live in the flesh does not necessarily mean living a life of debauchery and licence, it simply means living our lives according to our desires or thinking. One can live a very respectable life and still live in the flesh. We can be full of good works because we have set out to be a good person. To live in the spirit means to live by what God says. Jesus said that his words were spirit and they were life. That means if we obey what he says our spirit will come more alive and be more easily influenced by the Holy Spirit who dwells within us. It takes effort and discipline to live in our spirit because we are so used to living in our feelings or our reasonings. These are not wrong; they are simply unreliable and in the world of the spirit they are very inadequate.

Faith is a Gift

When we were baptized, we received the gift of faith; faith was infused into us. Infused faith is dormant faith, unconscious faith. Superimposing Christian doctrines on an unconscious faith does not necessarily bring it to life. When this happens all that results is that Christian truths and principles are instilled into the mind, and if we think knowing the teachings of the Church is the same as believing in them, then we are making a great mistake.

A person may go to church, may practise the faith without ever coming to a living faith in Jesus Christ and in what has been achieved by his death and resurrection. Knowing he died and rose again is not the same as trusting in those truths. Jesus promised to send his Holy Spirit who would remind us of all that Jesus had said and would lead us into truth. This leading into truth is not by way of deductive arguments, that is the way reason works; it is by illuminating our spirit, so that we know a truth clearly and yet are not able to say how or why we know it. But the knowing is certain; we would die for it.

When I say there is an illuminating, I do not mean that out of the blue we suddenly know a truth we did not know before, though God, of course, can make that happen. This illuminating tends to come, rather, while we are wrestling with doctrine or Scripture; in other words as we are searching, the Spirit enables us to find the truth. We do not reach it by our efforts, although our efforts are important and necessary, but the Holy Spirit enlightens us.

Gifts Need Receiving

Holiness is God's work, but if we do not co-operate with him, channelling into our lives what Jesus has achieved for us through his death and resurrection, then we will never know God's power to save (Romans 1:16). God the Father sent his Son to save us; God the Son willingly came to do that work; and God the Holy Spirit makes, from one generation to the next, the work of Jesus effective in those who believe in and co-operate with him.

Believing that it is God who saves us does not mean we just sit around and let him do it. There is much for us to do if we are going to allow God to save us, and our main job is to get out of the way so that the Holy Spirit may do his work. St Paul reminds us 'it is by grace you have been saved' (Ephesians 2:8) and yet, in another verse he tells us 'to work for our salvation "in fear and trembling" ' (Philippians 2:13).

A man who had a beautiful allotment was working there one day when a passer-by paused to admire the neat rows of vegetables bordered by flowers carefully chosen for their colour. 'My! Isn't God wonderful?' he said. The gardener straightened up agreeing that that was so and added, 'But you should have seen this place when he had it to himself!' It is God who gives the power of growth; gardeners, through their hard work, channel God's power into order and design.

What We Must Do

Having looked in a fair amount of detail at faith, we need now to ask ourselves if we tend to *have* faith rather than *live* faith. Living by faith is not easy; we have to learn how to do it. Since our baptism faith has been in us, but if we have not been accustomed to living by faith, we will not be able suddenly to start. Muscles that have been long neglected, cannot suddenly be expected to work with ease. There is no easy road back to full vigour without much effort and suffering. Faith is not contrary to reason, it is beyond it. We spend a lot of time developing our thinking faculties, and while this is important and very necessary, the fact remains true that the more we develop our reasoning processes and neglect to nourish our spirit, the harder it is to submit to faith.

We are created for God and our hearts are restless until they rest in him. Sin has darkened our minds to the truth and we imagine that we are created for self-fulfilment and when we hear that we are made for him, this can make us see God as a threat. Every approach he makes towards us rings alarm bells within us and, like Adam, we hide. Before we can reach that place where we dare to surrender to God, much work has to be done and it is a long painful process. Our many so-called conversions can sometimes only be us beginning to see God in a new way but we continue to seek him for ourselves. It can take a lifetime before God can get us into the place where we put down our defences, surrender unconditionally and seek him for himself.

When we declare that Jesus Christ is our Lord and Saviour we state clearly that our salvation does not depend on our work. Making such acts of faith enables the Spirit of God to effect in us what Jesus Christ has already achieved. This is what the doctrine of salvation by faith means. So through the sacraments and a life lived trusting in the Lord's achievements we can constantly be in contact with the Lord, receiving his power to live the new life.

For Reflection

- How do you think of faith? Is it intellectually assenting to doctrines, or a way of life for you?
- Do you see the difference between believing God exists and believing in God?
- Which would you choose among the following as essential for salvation? Belonging to the Roman Catholic Church? Belief in the existence of God? Going to Mass on Sundays and holidays of obligation? Living a good moral life? Belief in Jesus as Saviour through his death and resurrection?
- Do your failures make you feel separated from God? What do you do about them?
- How are you nourishing your belief in what God has revealed?
- Has Christianity become a 'religion' for you? Or is it a constant help and joy?
- Just where, in your list of priorities, does Jesus come? We all know where he should come, but where actually does he come? I am not talking about feelings, I am talking about facts. Surely the One who created us and died to save us, should come top. But is he at the top? If not, we should deliberately put him there. For me, that is to live by faith. This involves a very deliberate act of trust in what the Lord has done for me, a very deliberate act of thanksgiving, and doing these frequently during the busy day. It is a matter of habit and practice.

5

We Are Not Alone

Just as a human body, though it is made up of many parts, is a single unit because all these parts . . . make one body, so it is with Christ. (1 Corinthians 12:12)

Just as you cannot have a bonfire with just one branch, we in the church need one another to make us strong. God intended humankind to live as a family, but not a family on its own, rather as an extension of the family of the Trinity. Just as the Father is not the Son, and the Son is not the Spirit – they are three Persons forming one Godhead – so also the human family, made up as it is of many individuals, is intended to be linked together by the very fact that they each have a share in the divine life.

The Fall put an end to God's plan, but through the redemption won by his Son, we humans can share in the divine life, even here on earth, by receiving that life into our spirits. We still have our own individual life, but we are also given new life in Christ, and this means all those who share that new life, are linked together. The normal way that a person receives this new life is by being baptized into the Church. However, God is not bound by his own gifts and he can give this new life to those who, through no fault of their own, have not heard of baptism or have not understood its meaning, but in some way have recognized Jesus.

The point I want to make in this chapter is that if I share life with another I can both help or hinder that life and the same is true the other way round. Those who believe in Jesus do not just form a group with a common belief, they form a body, the body of the resurrected Christ who wishes to remain in the world so that he can serve his Father in us, and can minister to us through each other.

Just as the human body, though made up of many parts, forms one unit, so the human family was intended by God to be united. The parts of the human body are very different from each other, but all are needed to make one body. The hand cannot do the work of the liver, and the liver cannot do the work of the hand, but both are essential. Whereas in the human body individual parts cannot exist on their own, the human family is made up of persons with their own individual existence. This means our corporate unity is not so obvious.

When Jesus taught us to pray he did not tell us to say 'My Father . . . give me this day . . .'. In teaching us to say 'our' he was emphasizing the way God looks at his creation. He also taught that it was not possible to love God without loving our neighbour. We may well think that we are able to love God without loving our neighbour, but that is because we equate loving God with a feeling rather than seeing it as an act of the will to love God and all that he has made.

Sin blinds us. We were made for God and to be in harmony with one another. Sin makes us see everything from our own point of view, and this makes God and neighbour seem rather threatening because we view life from where we are, not from where God is. This again prompts the question, 'Who is this God that we are serving? Is he the real God or one of our own making?'

The tragedy is that the Church has become divided, and although we are in the process of getting back together, there are still innumerable, and at times seemingly insurmountable, obstacles. Even within the denominations there are divisions: there is high church, low church, Latin Mass societies, charismatic folk groups, traditionalists, conservatives. What should be uniting us together is not a liking for this or that, rather it should be a concern to see Christ proclaimed. We all have our likes and dislikes, and it is tragic when we divide over them.

'See these Christians, how they love one another'. I fear we are a long way from that. The world has never yet seen true unity, except perhaps during the very first few days after Pentecost when everyone pooled their belongings – but quite soon the whole question of whether or not believers should be circumcised came up and from there on many different opinions began to be aired and this faction appeared against that one. Christian history is not something to be proud of, but perhaps, when true unity is achieved, the world will then believe. I wonder how far we have actually gone ecumenically? Do we in general think it a good thing that Christians should be united, or deep down are there still unnamed anxieties and suspicions? Loyalty to a denomination can be a defence against ecumenism, but how united are we with those with whom we worship Sunday after Sunday? Do we really see that we have a life in common and that my spiritual life can affect another? How anxious are we, I wonder, to see Christ formed in each other?

I believe it is possible to be more Catholic than Christian, and when that happens we lose sight of the good news and we are in danger of finding 'religion'. The question I have been concentrating on in this book is, how does the gospel appear to us? Is it a matter of rules and regulations, or is it the good news of God redeeming all of us? The Word of

88

God can so easily become rules for life and not a life-giving rule. The Lord is not giving us numerous precepts to obey, but rather actual facts for us to believe to enable us to receive life.

We have great power for each other and that power can reach to the ends of the earth. I always find it inspiring to think that men and women choose to live a life of prayer by joining an enclosed order. On the face of it, one may wonder what use such a life is; but if we dig deeper we can see the unique gift of a community of people belonging to each other. No doubt such an existence could become a bolt hole for those who cannot face life, but such motives should be spotted and dealt with. I thank God that while I am working in a parish or in a retreat centre, there are those who by their prayers are causing floods of grace to minister to me and those whom I am serving. Being in Christ needs to become a reality to us. At the beginning of the Eucharist the Church asks us to confess to each other, as well as God, our failures. We need to ask each other for forgiveness for often being a slack cell in the Body of Christ.

It is perhaps helpful to remember that elsewhere in the world at this very moment there are people facing crises – perhaps they are being persecuted for their faith or undergoing a crisis of belief, and are in need of strength. We can help them from where we are by being that healthy cell. If we are praising God for who he is and thanking him for what he has done, then we are praying that his kingdom, which is already among us, may have its full effect. We can ask God to direct his victory to whoever is in need. How important it is that we are vibrantly believing people, confident that the Lord is with us and his victory, already won, is being worked out in time and place. The trouble is we do not see or perceive with our minds the invisible, and thus we fail to believe. We need to lift up our eyes, to be brave and believe.

Even in the natural order we need one another. No one is self-sufficient. Not everyone is to be a farmer; not everyone is to be a dentist; not everyone is to be a builder. Each person has his or her own talent which is to be used for the good of the whole. We call this invisible family 'society' and its members are called not to live for themselves alone but for the good of the whole. It is sad when today such pressure is put on people to get what they can out of life, for they can then lose the sense of the larger family. If you add to this invisible family a common shared life, you begin to see something of what Church means. We are bound together, not just as members of the human family, but also as sharers in a common divine life.

Eve was given as a helpmate to Adam, the Church

is the helpmate to Christ. He has won the victory, and our task is to ask for it to be applied here, there and everywhere. If we are immersed in our own problems and worries, then we become a dead cell in the Body of Christ, and when there are many dead cells, then the Body is sick.

Sin divided creation – Adam blamed Eve; Eve blamed the serpent. Deep down in each of us there exists a drive to preserve self. We can even seek God for ourselves. We would like to be thought holy, because we misunderstand and think holiness is our achievement, and we want to be admired for reaching such heights. Holiness is not reaching heights, it is accepting our poverty.

I believe that any life that seeks to avoid others needs careful examining. Some are called to be hermits, but not so as to avoid others, but rather to serve others through sacrifice and worship of God. We must remember that other people are other people and it is not wrong to be other. My hand is not my ear, and thank God for that. You are not me; and thank God for that.

God's plan is that we share new life in Christ and for this to happen effectively, each must surrender his or her own life. Too often we try to blend in with others, hoping their plans will not interfere too much with ours. I think we have to do something much more positive, we are not called just to adjust to others but to live for others. If everyone lived for the other, we would all get loved. If we all wait to be loved, then we might end up waiting for evermore. If we all decide to love, then we will get loved.

Love is not a matter of feeling, it is a matter that concerns the will. It is a decision. We need to pray that our vision will be extended outside ourselves so that we become acutely aware of this invisible family. We live in a world that stresses the individual; we are encouraged to 'spoil' ourselves. Such encouragement can appeal to our fallen nature which tends to look inward and to see others only as a possible means of advancement.

I see this as a problem which does not just affect individuals, it also affects nations. Very often what advances one country is literally killing many others by making their peoples live in poverty and slavery. We, alas, do not see it until some good Samaritan brings it to our notice. Thank God for those who make us aware of the injustices that we quite often unconsciously inflict on others in poorer parts of the world.

Love, though, is not just a matter of our decision for that presumes we are capable of loving. We are capable of loving only because the Holy Spirit has been poured into our hearts; but the Holy Spirit does not take us over and fill us with so much love that we have to act. No, the action has to come from us first. Peter did not wait until he was certain he could walk on the water, he launched out and then found the power. We also have to launch out and then we find the power. The launching is what is so difficult, because not feeling very loving, it is hard to love; but once we take the step then the love, poured into us by the Holy Spirit, is tapped and the miracle happens.

The world has never yet seen true unity and that is why, when it happens, it will be recognized as the work of God. Only God can make one out of two. Often the union of Christ with his Church has been likened to a marriage where two become one flesh. It is alarming to think what sins are being tolerated today, even by those who call themselves ministers, against this sacred command of God for unity.

For Reflection

- Do we see other Christians as other people or people with whom we actually share divine life?
- How do we view other denominations? Do they frighten us? Threaten us? Make us feel uncertain?
- Do we really want unity among Christians? Jesus prayed for unity (John 17).
- We may not be able to see how it can come about, but do we desire to see it happen?

The Faith Journey

'I am the light of the world; anyone who follows me will not be walking in the dark; he will have the light of life.'

(John 7:12)

Seeking God is not the same as being found by God. Yet it is not our seeking God that gets us found; rather it is our discovery that despite our seeking we cannot find him, that puts us in the place where, if we dare to wait, we can be found. But seek we must.

In this chapter I want to talk about the ongoing journey and our search for God, about how we reach a point where things become dark and difficult and how this is usually the point where growth occurs if we persevere. Some writers call it 'the dark night of the soul', others 'mystic death'. It does not really matter what it is called: what is important is to acknowledge its existence.

It is always God who moves first and he starts us on our search by attracting us. I believe it is crucial to understand that God makes this first move. It took me a long time to grasp this and I fear I was introduced to mystic death before I had found the God of laughter and joy. To be taught to wait for God before you know something of the one you are waiting for is a recipe for failure. Boredom will drive you to search in the wrong places for answers.

I think it was the Benedictine monk, John Main, who said that if we had the choice of listening to a talk on prayer for half an hour, or reading a book on prayer for half an hour, or going and praying for half an hour, most of us would choose either the talk or the book. I wonder why? Maybe the reason is because none of us is satisfied with our prayer and we are always hopeful that we might improve it. The whole point of prayer is to make us meet our poverty, and thus gradually to wean us from ourselves. Searching for 'more successful' methods can be part of the endless search for self-satisfaction and can thus defeat the whole prayer encounter.

Sin has deeply wounded us and can make our noble efforts to search for God a disguised search for self. I wonder if our disenchantment at seeing how we really are could be God's way of getting us to abandon ourselves into his hands? Any sense that we are getting somewhere might enmesh us more and more in self. Prayer is a place where I meet my poverty.

God in his mercy does not plunge us into an experience of poverty right at the beginning. He starts by attracting us, and very often that attraction comes through our senses. Beauty in all its forms, whether visible or audible, lifts us up. Colour, clouds, spring flowers, wild seascapes have profound effects on us humans and in some way we feel we touch God through them.

The Church uses sign, music, ceremony to help us as we pray to the God who cannot be captured by any of these things. These ways by which God begins to attract us must not be despised. For myself, I think I was introduced to the God of darkness before I had met the God of light. I loved creation but I failed to see God in it – because what I met in creation bore little resemblance to the God I learnt about in church who seemed gloomy and forbidding; certainly he was not associated in my mind with colour, light and beauty.

Creation tells us something about God, but it does not bring us into contact with the person of God. For that to happen we need to hear God speak. We cannot spend our lives in our senses; besides, what once moved us profoundly can one day cease to have that effect on us. It is sad when we go chasing after the latest experience of God, when none of these things can contain him.

Sooner or later God will see fit to move us on in our search of him. Learning that God has spoken to us and has a plan, half of which is already achieved, can now begin to capture our minds. How sad it is when at this stage we meet with those who teach us wrongly about God. That is why it is so important to hear what God has said about himself and his plans for us. How I thank God for the Catholic Church for I know I can get sound teaching and revelation, but I also realize that not every teacher in the Church follows the teachings of the universal Church. At one time I did not recognize that, and that led to much confusion on my part.

As our minds begin to be involved, we move from the wonder of God who manifests something of himself in the beauty of creation, to meet the One who so loved us he became one of us so that he could pay for our faults. With awe and wonder we begin to absorb all that God has done for us.

Our prayer at this time relies less on feelings and is more caught up with facts. We become anxious to hear more and more of God's Word. In one sense our prayer time is quite active for we are desirous to learn more and more of the wonder of God's love for us. Many stray thoughts suddenly tie together. Of course, as in the time when our senses were more involved, there are ups and downs. Sometimes we seem to be aware of many new insights, at other times we feel heavy and slow.

Sooner or later the question has to be faced: do I like praying for what I get out of it, or do I really want to give God glory? Slowly, but gradually, God begins to get us out of the driving seat. He now begins to take over and direct things his way. This is a time of crisis because we start to feel a total failure and what was once rather fruitful can now seem so barren. What is happening is that God is beginning to direct the operation. Up to now we have been very much in charge and therefore able to take credit for what has been achieved.

It is most distressing to begin to see what we are really like. We can resist the process but that will only prolong it. We need to be shown what we are really like and admit it for ourselves. It is the beginning of a deep purification.

This, alas, is the moment when many people give up prayer and substitute it with either work or 'prayers'. I really do not think it is much help to be told that from now on prayer will be difficult and it is just a question of hanging on in there. We need to be told what is happening.

The journey we are on is not a journey of advancing along a way, it is the journey of the caterpillar into a butterfly. I am sure the caterpillar does not decide when to become a chrysalis. Somewhere in our journey we have to give up being in the driving seat and allow another to take over. Alas it does not appear that simple when it starts to happen. To the one undergoing this change everything seems to be collapsing. It would be a comfort if we knew God was taking over, but we do not understand what is happening.

The truth is we are extremely attached to ourselves, and God's way of detaching us is to make us thoroughly dissatisfied with ourselves. It is one thing to practise humility, quite another to see ourselves as we truly are.

This is the mystical dying which comes to all of us in God's own time. Up until this period we have done our penances, our self-denials, our acts of humility. These are all good and right, but they are not the real thing. There is a difference between acting in a humble way and being humble. When God begins to act, then we are no longer the one who decides. This is a time of crisis; are we ready to give unconditional surrender?

The old man in us prevents the new man being formed by trying to become the new man by self-effort. Here again we meet the challenge: will it be God's way or our way? There has to come a time when effort to renew ourselves ceases, and is replaced by willingness to allow ourselves to be renewed. It is a question of letting go, of learning to hand over, something we find very difficult to do. Transformation can only happen in us through mystic death and, even though we may long to be renewed, we cannot bring it about; all we can do is to choose to stand in the desert and wait in barrenness, thus allowing our senses and mind to be put to death, emptying ourselves and turning to God imploring him to enter in and transform us. This entering is spiritual, our senses and mind are not involved. This waiting appears to be a complete waste of time, but that is what mystic death is like; it is death to self, and involves standing and waiting, unaware that the One who died and rose again is at work applying his death to us so that we might rise with him to a new way of living.

As the Holy One enters, he purifies, and as we allow him entrance, emptying ourselves to allow him room, so we become filled with him causing our fine human qualities of love, gentleness and concern to be empowered with his new life so that even our very actions become outward expressions of him who is holy.

It really is not within the scope of this book to chart this part of the journey in great detail. Many fine books have been written on the subject. My object has been to lay the foundations, so that a person may arrive at this stage, where God begins to take over.

Of course the whole journey has been God's work, but like the gardener we have had much preparation to do. My main object has been to expose the false ideas of God which require us to reform ourselves and thus enter into his kingdom through our own power. I have wanted to replace Satan's lie with the tremendous truth that God loved us so much that he sent his Son to bear our sins and to give us a share in his resurrected life enabling us to live in a new way. The odd thing is that even though it is God's work, he does reward us, as though it was we who achieved it. The truth really does set us free. God has given us the truth, we must listen to it, hear it, accept it and act on it, and then experience its power to set us free (see John 8:31–2).

For Reflection

- Love is a journey out of self into another. Because of sin, we tend to journey into ourselves. It is only by the power of the cross that we can die to self and truly journey into God. So do not be discouraged at finding prayer difficult. Prayer is not about having heavenly sensations; it is standing in poverty before the One who loves us. It is not easy to stand in poverty; we wish to stand with some successes to our name.

- When all seems dark, it is not necessarily our fault. Perhaps God is purifying us by showing us our poverty.

- There are many books on this subject, but what

helps one does not necessarily help another. Remember we are ambitious creatures, and we even want to succeed in spiritual things; so be on your guard against wanting to seem to make progress. People can become fascinated with 'spiritual nights', and such things can be signs of an ego trip. Finding a good spiritual guide to help us on our journey is important, especially when things seem to become difficult.

- *Love is a journey out of self into another. Because of sin we tend to journey into ourselves. It is only by the power of the cross that we die to self and truly journey into God.*

Your Sins
Are
Forgiven

Acknowledgements

The Scripture quotations in this publication are from *The Jerusalem Bible* and *The New Jerusalem Bible*, both published and copyright by Darton, Longman and Todd Ltd and Doubleday and Co. Inc. Excerpts from the English translation of *The Roman Missal* are copyright 1973, International Committee on English in the Liturgy, Inc. All rights reserved.

Introduction

This book is not a theological treatise on the sacrament of reconciliation, it is rather what one pilgrim, over many years, has come to understand and has found helpful, after much wrestling and searching. My insights are my insights, I trust they are also the Church's, and I offer them in simple language. In doing so, I know I run the risk of being misunderstood. I prefer to do this, though, rather than have everything so doctrinally perfect that the ordinary person cannot understand it.

At one time confession (now called the sacrament of reconciliation) was a regular occurrence in the life of most Catholics; but since Vatican II it has become far less frequent for many, and for others has altogether ceased.

There are many reasons for this. I feel one of the main ones is the failure to relate the sacrament to the redemption already won by the Lord. Perhaps too much emphasis has been put on sacraments and not enough on the Lord who touches us through them.

I, certainly, misunderstood the Catholic teachings that I received and it was only through a crisis of faith that I discovered what being a Catholic really meant. Through counselling many people, I have discovered that my misunderstandings are quite common. I have therefore written this book in the hope that one man's struggles, questionings and ponderings, might be of some help to others.

In confession one meets very complex problems to which there often seem no legitimate solutions, and a priest is faced with both exercising the mercy of God and seeing that sanctions are not given to a state of living which is forbidden by God. I confess I shall not be dealing with such complex problems in this book; rather my reason for writing is to help very ordinary people find, or refind, the extra-ordinary power of this sacrament, not just to forgive sins, but also to free us from them.

1

Misunderstandings

 Truths are not just for learning, we have to dare to live them and thus discover that they are true. This is a risky business because they may be found wanting. Our temptation is to keep them as truths known but untried. Who can describe the utter panic one experiences when the rock on which one stands suddenly appears to be made of sand.

We have all got our stories, mine is one among millions, neither better nor worse. I have no real answers, and I am beginning to realise that knowing answers is not that important. What is important is that I am asked to believe that I am loved beyond measure and have been bought at a terrible price. All my training to be successful, to master my life, cries out against such a truth, because popular belief teaches that we are valued by what we do and not by what we are. In thinking, we try to master situations, for we imagine that when we know, then we are in control. How difficult it is to surrender, yet surrendering will be the greatest thing we ever do.

There is no guarantee, even if the truth has been well taught, that it will have been learnt correctly. Communication is not that simple. People hear what they hear, and they will put their own inter-pretation on it. I am still amazed, even alarmed, at my own misunderstandings of what I was taught. I do not accuse any of my teachers of teaching me wrongly. I heard what they said, but I coloured it with what was already in my mind. I could even answer correctly the questions put to me, but I now see that those answers were not my answers, I was only giving back what I had heard. I have often said that I would like to have repeated my theology several years after I had been ordained a priest – then I would have had real questions needing real answers.

It was only at a time of crisis that I discovered that many of the truths that I had learnt from others were, in fact, just other people's answers, and they had not become my answers. In other words I was living on what others had said and was now ques-tioning whether I really believed the answers I had been given. It was not that I disbelieved them, I had only accepted them intellectually and did not actively live by them. I do not think there is any-thing very shocking in that. The trouble is that truth can often remain as something learnt and does not become something believed in.

As a priest I have counselled many people and I have found immense ignorance with regard to the basic message of the gospel. My experience was the same, so I am not surprised at it. It is quite understandable for often when we were being taught these truths, religion was not our most popular subject, and from a career point of view, it was not the most important. Bits of information were picked up and the final picture often bore little resemblance to the truth.

To illustrate what I mean, imagine someone who has never seen anyone play golf. Perhaps his first reaction at seeing someone hit a ball, would be one of marvel and amazement that such a small ball could be hit with such an odd-looking instrument. What skill, he would think to himself! He may even be tempted to have a go, and so he buys a club and some balls. His first attempts are disastrous: try as he might he cannot manage to hit the ball. Finally he buys a book and slowly learns about keeping one's eye on the ball, how to hold the club, how to stand. In time he becomes quite proficient and is able to hit the ball a fair distance in the right direction. But he cannot be called a golfer, because he has not yet learnt the point of hitting the ball – no one has told him that he has to get the ball into the hole in the least number of shots. It is true that he has become quite expert at part of the game. The same can happen with the gospel – we can become quite proficient at part of the gospel, but if we have never learnt its heart, then we only know part of the message. In order to understand the Church and its practices and ceremonies, we need to know and understand the mission of Jesus Christ.

I wonder if, after the Reformation, priests and teachers of the Catholic faith reacted to what the Protestants were protesting about, and began putting a strong emphasis on some of those very doctrines that caused dissension, with the result that the Eucharist, confession, Mary and purgatory received special attention. Over a long period of time this could produce people who were more steeped in Catholic doctrine than they were in basic Christian beliefs. Nothing has actually been denied, it just means not enough has been taught.

I was in that boat – I knew part of the gospel but the very core was missing. It is not surprising if any who have had the same experience do not understand the Church's practices; they lack a true understanding of the mission of Jesus Christ.

As I grew up 'grace' was something I heard much about. In many ways it is not a good word because it is a neuter and grace becomes thought of as an 'it'. True, it does mean 'gift', but to a young child that is not obvious. I thought of grace as being like spiritual petrol enabling me to do good things, and it was always wise to make sure your tank was fairly full of it, just in case death should intervene. Sin, rather like dirt in a petrol tank, stopped grace from acting efficiently – though I confess I was not too sure how all that worked. What was clear was that the sacrament of confession was important because, in some way, it removed the bad effects of sin and gave me more grace.

Grace was significant and it seemed that I had to get as much of it as I could. With this emphasis on 'grace', I can now see that I came to imagine that 'grace' would save me and so I had to try and acquire as much as possible. My mind was locked into this idea and everything was coloured by it. What a crisis I went through when I began to see that it was Jesus who saved and not grace. I felt very akin to Luther and really understood for the first time what 'salvation by faith' meant. I was suddenly faced with the question, 'Was the Church of Rome right or wrong?'

I am not someone who makes quick decisions so I did not go rushing out of the Church. I did spend some miserable years trying to sort myself and the Church out. Was I too Catholic in my upbringing? How could I have missed the gospel message? Slowly, gradually and painfully my mind began to clear and I could see I had laid too much stress on grace and sacraments instead of on the Lord. How important it was that I went through that crisis for I can now see the riches of the Church with clearer eyes. I see the sacraments as very much part of the Lord's plan, but I can also see that if we are not taught carefully what the Lord did for us, then sacraments can become substitutes for God.

I have counselled enough people to know that my experience is not unique and it was this that prompted me to write the book *This is My Body* in which I showed that the Mass continues in us the work that Christ has already completed on Calvary. I see sacraments as making present in us what the Lord has already done. Many people have dropped going to confession. Once it was greatly used, maybe over-used, but what a loss it is not to see how great a gift is offered us. I hope my thoughts, my mistakes and my misunderstandings may help some to re-find this gift that God has given to us.

2

Sin – What Is It?

We may wonder how these misunderstandings happen. There are several reasons, some natural, others spiritual. To pass a truth on to another person is not that simple. Each of us is individual and through a whole series of events and circumstances we pick up impressions and feelings, and we interpret what we hear according to what life has taught us. Words, meaning one thing for the speaker, may evoke something very different for the listener and this is bound to colour the way in which they are heard.

What is more important, and in spite of opinions held today we must not forget it, is that there is a deceiver, Satan – known as the father of lies. We can be sure that he is very anxious that we do not hear the truth, or, if we do hear it, that we will misunderstand it, for it would be a very real threat to his kingdom if we became convinced of the truth.

There is a battle going on for our mind. Whatever gets into our mind is either filed away in the memory or is acted upon. There is an evil power anxious to fill our minds with untruth.

We were made by God and for God (Col. 1:16). This means that our complete fulfilment will be found in living and existing totally for God. Free will is not the liberty to do what we want, it is the liberty to do willingly what we were made for. So for us humans, the peak of our contentment is willingly existing for God.

In the Fall, through a series of subtle deceptions, Adam and Eve freely chose not to live for God, but to live for themselves, making their own decisions as to what is good or evil. Today much time and energy is spent in arguing about exactly what happened at the Fall, and all this seems to do is to keep us from admitting the fact of the Fall itself and from acknowledging the nature of original sin.

Quite starkly, sin is our refusal to admit that God is God and that we are his creatures; it is our bid for independence, our bid to say we are God, not just made in his image. It is a deep rebellion of the creature against the Creator; a refusal to serve or obey. When God is made to appear as a rival, then he appears demanding, threatening, out-there, against us, opposite, and we fear him. We become suspicious of his promises, and these now appear as punishments or threats, and he who is all good is not trusted by us for he seems to our distorted vision to be dangerous.

What a distortion of the truth this is! When we speak of a 'darkened mind' this is what we mean: God who is all good appears to us as a threat. Many, many people see God in these terms. Usually they will not admit to such thoughts, and so these thoughts have gone into the unconscious and may only surface at a time of crisis. But how is it that God is seen in such a way? We need to remember that there is an enemy within, a fifth columnist, who plays on our fallen nature whispering untruths to us, appealing to our desire for freedom, liberty and self-expression.

We did not become sinners the day we committed our first sin; we were born sinners. It is not by sinning that we become sinners; we sin because we *are* sinners. This truth is clearly taught by the Church and by Scripture, yet how few people really know it. Today, there is a move to talk about 'original blessings' rather than 'original sin' – another example of our rebellion against the truth. In history there have been those who have ranted and raged giving us the impression that human nature is sin-soaked, and it may be in reaction to this sort of thinking that we now prefer to talk of blessings. Original sin is a fact, but that does not mean that sin is intrinsic to human nature. The incarnation is proof of that. Let there be no mistake, if we play down original sin, we play down the need for redemption.

God's plan was that we should be in his Son. He planned this from all eternity. 'Before the world was made, he chose us, chose us in Christ, to be holy and spotless . . . for his own kind purposes' (Eph. 1:4–5). The Fall was not in his plan; the Fall came about through our free will. But God's plan has not changed; rather, he has had to take the Fall into account. In this sense we can talk about the 'original blessing', which is still God's plan, but to harp back to that, ignoring that there was a Fall, is a failure to see things as they are.

Sin blinds us

Jesus told us that his Spirit would show the world how wrong it is about sin. If you ask people what they think sin is, you will see how right Jesus was. You will hear many different opinions and I imagine hardly anyone will say that sin is our refusal to admit that God is God, our refusal to believe in him and in what he has done through his Son's death and resurrection.

I know a priest who asked someone, confined to their home through sickness, if they would like to go to confession and he was told: 'But, father, I never go out of the house.' Sin for that person was something that happened outside, in the street or somewhere but not at home.

I once upset two ladies by saying in a talk that death was the penalty for sin. They came to me at the end of the talk feeling quite hurt over this statement. In the course of talking it came out that their brother had died two months previously and 'he was no sinner. Why, he hever harmed anybody.' Sin for them was something public involving scandal, physical harm or harm to someone's property.

If we are going to profit from looking at the sacrament where sin is both forgiven and taken away, then it is important that we try to grasp what sin really is. This is difficult because sin makes us less and less aware of spiritual realities. It is like a drug, it dulls our perception of the truth. Kierkegaard once said: 'To have a weak understanding of sin is part of our being a sinner.' If you want advice about a colour scheme, it is best not to ask someone who is colour blind. Or if you want advice about a certain recording machine, do not ask someone who is tone-deaf. So, if we want to know about sin, do not ask a sinner. Only God can tell us what sin is.

Sin hides itself

Psalm 35 (36) says: 'Sin speaks to the sinner in the depth of his heart' – dulling his awareness of the real situation – 'he flatters himself in his mind that he knows not his guilt.' How important for Satan that we do not know our real sin. The very fact that so many are quite unaware of the sin in their lives, shows how the devil really has a trump card in making us so dull-witted with regard to it. Obviously, none of us is so foolish as to say that we are without sin, but we fondly think that we are all right. After all, we go to church, we live respectable lives, we are nice and we really harm no one.

I once heard a retreat-giver read 1 Corinthians 13, substituting the word 'gentleman' for the word 'love': 'A gentleman is always patient and kind; a gentleman is never jealous; a gentleman is not boastful or conceited . . .' The implication clearly was that Christianity is about decency and good manners.

Our originating sin has warped us and we want to live for ourselves. Long before any actual sin gets committed there is a rebellious disposition within us. We are all impregnated with the attitude 'I will not serve'.

17

Sins of injustice

Today sin is often seen as offences against human-kind and there is a tremendous awareness of the terrible injustices being committed all over the world. With the rapid progress of communication, we are able to see in our homes, through television, whatever has happened in the world. Visual communication is very powerful and how marvellous to see historic occasions taking place before our own eyes, or to get caught up in tension-filled moments as we watch teams battling for victory in some sport. But also many horrific scenes are brought into our living rooms and people are becoming more and more aware of the injustices that are being done. There are now many movements for righting the shameful way that the rich nations of the world have bled the poor ones. It was remarkable how the pop stars were able to raise so much money for the starving in Ethiopia, and I felt encouraged that there was a world-wide act of caring.

We are in an age when people's rights are very much to the fore, and again I cannot but rejoice as I see the concern for justice and fair play becoming so important to large numbers of people. Is the world then becoming more humane?

Humanism, however, must not be seen as the same as Christianity. It is not the same because humanism puts the human being in the centre of the stage, whereas Christianity puts Christ there. While many are asserting their rights or clamouring for the rights of this group or that, we need to ask who is clamouring for the rights of God?

So, in summing up this chapter I state again that

sin is the refusal to let God be God; a refusal to accept our state as creature, and we do this because of our darkened mind. St Paul, in his letter to the Romans, singles out *the* sin as this refusal to acknowledge God as God. It is not denying that God exists, it is rather choosing to ignore him that is so evil. It is the refusal on the part of the creature to be creature. It is the repeat of the human being's original sin: 'I will not serve'.

If God can be moved off the scene, then of course all his rights would disappear also. The original sin of humankind was to refuse to acknowledge God as master.

Abortionists claim that we have a right over life and the life of an unwanted child can be terminated at will. It is no longer what God sees as right, it is what the human sees as right.

I once heard someone say that *the* sin was all the injustices that the first world commits against the third world. While I do not deny the gravity of this sin, or in any way belittle its seriousness by what I now say, I would claim that *the* sin is the failure of Christians to live the heart of the gospel. If we fail to believe really in the power of the Cross of Jesus to save us from sin, then of course we will fall into sins of injustice and thoughtlessness, especially when they can so easily be hidden from our eyes. Trying to right the injustices of this world can end up in another attempt to solve the problems of the world by human power alone and not by what God has already done through Jesus Christ.

If our minds have been so blinded, what are we to do? We need a lamp for our steps and God in his mercy has provided that lamp. He has done an amazing thing and in order to benefit, we need to know what he has done and to accept it by putting our trust in his plan.

3

God's Remedy

 When our vision of God is wrong, we tend to think that it is God who must change and not we ourselves. I doubt, though, if we would own up to thinking that way, because we are masters at deceiving ourselves.

Our eyes are made to function in the light, and so the light is a delight to them. If we damage our eyes, then the light, once a delight, becomes painful to us. It is not the light that has changed, it is our eyes that have changed, and our eyes that need healing.

In the last chapter we saw that we were made *by* God and *for* God and that meant our greatest joy and delight was to live and exist for him. But sin has warped our vision of God, darkening our mind and instead of perceiving him as he really is, he now appears threatening, demanding and someone to fear. It is not that God has changed, it is we who have changed and it is we who are in need of healing.

In St Matthew's Gospel Jesus says that when salt loses its saltiness it is no longer good for anything and it can only be thrown out (5:13). Sin has seriously wounded human nature and to our darkened eyes the all good God appears menacing and threatening. Is it possible to cure the human family of this sickness, or like the unsalty salt, should we be discarded? When cattle get foot-and-mouth disease, they can only be wiped out and a fresh start has to be made. Can the human family, which was made to be God-centred, be cured of the besetting sin of self-centredness? God has come up with a solution which does involve a wiping out and making a fresh start, but the way he does this is wonderful to behold.

God prepares his people

The Old Testament tells the drama of how God constantly woos the people he has chosen as his own. Time and again he has to chastise them, they then repent and he forgives, and this story is repeated over and over again. 'I did forsake you for a brief moment but in great compassion I shall take you back. In a flood of anger, for a moment I hid my face from you' (Isa. 54:7,8).

People worry about the God of the Old Testament who seems to get incredibly angry, but we must remember we are trying to express in human language a God who is beyond our wildest dreams or ideas. It would be terrible if God just did not care what happened to us; the very fact that he reacts to our foolish ways, shows how much he cares. Listen to any parent who is ticking their child off for running out into a road without looking; there will be plenty of anger in their reprimand. The reason for this is they love the child and are angry because the child exposed itself to danger and hurt. Sin harms *us*, not God, and God does not want us damaged by it, hence he reacts.

At times, it does appear as if God is ready to give up his chosen people. We read in Hosea: 'My people are bent on disregarding me; if they are summoned to come up, not one of them makes a move.' Try and imagine what distress that caused God. Yet he cannot bring himself to forsake his chosen ones.

> Ephraim, how could I part with you?
> Israel, how could I give you up?
> How could I make you like Admah
> or treat you like Zeboiim?
> My heart within me is overwhelmed,
> fever grips my inmost being.
> I will not give rein to my fierce anger,
> I will not destroy Ephraim again,
> for I am God, not man,
> the Holy One in your midst,
> and I shall not come to you in anger. (11:7–9)

All the sacrifices of the Old Testament involved an animal being put to death by having its throat cut, causing its blood to flow out and death to follow. The life of the animal is offered in reparation for human sin. The sacrifice was not able to atone for human sin, but it was a gesture and was a foreshadowing of the sacrifice that one day *would* atone for sin.

The life offered on the cross was the sinless, inno-cent life of the God-man and the laying down of this life was a perfect act of obedience so as to make up for all the disobedience of the human family. Adam's disobedience caused such untold damage, now the obedience of the God-man has healed that wound.

If any wish to benefit from this action of Jesus, they need to be told clearly what Jesus has done for them and they need to accept it willingly by being baptised into Christ.

God's remedy

God's plan to restart the human family without actually wiping out the old race is marvellous in the extreme. He sends his Son, the second person of the Blessed Trinity, to become a member of the human family. Through the overshadowing of the virgin Mary by the Holy Spirit, a child is conceived who is both Son of Man and Son of God. As Son of Man he can legitimately represent the human family; as Son of God, whatever action he does will have immense value because it will be an action done by God.

God's plan is that this beloved Son of his should bear in himself the consequences of all the sins of the human race. Through the incarnation, he has become a member of the human family; through his being baptised by John the Baptist, he has made solidarity with the fallen race, for John's baptism was a baptism of repentance. The innocent Jesus had no need to repent, but he wanted to be baptised into union with sinful men and women and take onto himself their sins.

To have enlightened understanding about the Passion of the Lord and to grasp truly what was going on, we will need much more than human skill or reason. Paul himself tells us that God's way of achieving our salvation appears folly to human reckoning (1 Cor. 1:21). It is the Spirit of God who reveals truths beyond human reason to our spirit (1 Cor. 2:14).

As we have seen, it was through disobedience that our minds have become darkened. God's extra-ordinary plan is that his Son should become so identified with sinners that he should experience this darkness himself, and yet continue to obey. In 2 Corinthians Paul says: 'God made the sinless one into sin' (5:21). What can that possibly mean? Countless Christians have pondered this text and after many years of wrestling with it I share my limited understanding.

In wanting his Son to stand in for the sins of the human race, the Father was asking something that no mere human could do. No ordinary human being could take on the sins of another, let alone the sins of all the world. But, Jesus is an absolutely unique man; he is both man and God. As God, the Creator, he has a deeper solidarity with the whole human family than any human being could have, and as man he can act in the name of humankind.

The plan of the Father, willingly accepted by Jesus, is for Jesus to experience the separation from God that sin causes. John Saward, in his beautiful book *The March Mysteries*, suggests that when Jesus cried out, 'My God, why have you forsaken me?' he was not giving into despair, rather he was crying out his acceptance of this place of dereliction which he willingly bore in the name of all. Jesus drinks deeply in obedience the bitter cup of separation and experiences the terror of being without the Father. No amount of imagining can plumb the depth of this pain. Beyond the excruciating agony of crucifixion, the Son of God, the closest to the Father, experiences the loss of the Father, and this is all the more painful because it is so undeserved.

At one time, and this shows how our darkened minds work, I thought Jesus was in some way making reparation for us by placating his Father's anger over our sin. I saw him as volunteering to accept the Father's punishment for us. But this puts Jesus and the Father in opposition to each other. Sin does not damage God, it damages us. It is not God who has fallen out with us, it is we who have fallen out with him, and it is we who need healing. Sin has made us disobedient, self-centred creatures. Jesus wishes to step in to where sin has landed us, and willingly to bear these consequences. By that act of obedience he undoes all our acts of disobedience. Adam, the head of the human family, disobeyed while living in a harmonious world; Jesus, the God-man, obeys while living in a world of disharmony.

Far from the idea of Jesus making satisfactory reparation, the Father's plan is one of sheer love. He was willing to allow his own beloved, innocent Son, to be besmirched with our sins and experience the terrible consequences of death and separation, *but* the Father knew the Son, as God, could not be swallowed up by death, and obedient unto the end, he would await the Father's command to rise up out of death. What a cost to both the Father and the Son – both were anxious and willing, even impatient, to accomplish such a plan. 'It was for this very reason that I have come to this hour' (John 12:27).

What love is shown by the Father in surrendering his Son; what love is shown by the Son in exposing himself to such a trial and in commending himself into the hands of his Father who, at that moment, seemed anything but Father. We cannot begin to fathom what it meant for the Son to embrace forsakenness. He endured abandonment for us, standing where the worst sinner would stand and lovingly accepting the consequence of every sin. For love of humankind, God wanted to experience the absence of God – and for him who is the very Word of God, such desolation far exceeds anything that a mortal human being could tolerate or bear. Only God can experience total abandonment. The plan is terrible, but the Son's willing obedience brings healing to the family of the human race.

As with all gifts, two steps are involved: there is a giving and there must be a receiving. We have looked at the giving, now we must turn our attention to the receiving. God has done a very costly thing for us. How tragic, if, through ignorance or a darkened mind, we fail to know the truth and never become set free.

How God's Remedy Reaches Us Through the Church

What Jesus has achieved needs to be made available to all generations who come after him. God does this by the means of his Church. The Church is Christ, through the Holy Spirit, continuing his work of rescue among us who come after his time here on earth. The Church is to teach God's truth and minister the redeeming work of Jesus.

I suppose all of us have on some occasion wished that we had lived at the time of Christ. Naively we imagine that we would have seen Jesus as we now see him, and therefore think we would have been on his side, forgetting that now we have the benefit of years of history that have shaped our understanding. Jesus would undoubtedly have challenged us just as he challenged the Jews of his time. We, like them, would have been starting from scratch, trying to make out who he was, knowing that he was not one of the official rabbis. This would have meant having to work through a lot of suspicion. His teaching was very challenging and he supported it by extraordinary miracles. I think the experience would have been very unnerving.

The Jews had been carefully taught that there was only one God, and believed the Jewish God was the only God. The surrounding nations believed in many gods and the chosen people were unique in their belief in one God. When Jesus came among them working extraordinary signs, and claiming to be the Son of God, this offended their beliefs and immediately made them suspicious of him.

If I try and imagine myself as one of the crowd listening to Jesus, I can see myself wanting to play it safe and being slow to come out on his side. There was so much against him that there were good reasons for hesitating, yet what he did and said was very challenging. It would have been very tempting to play it safe and leave one's options open. The book of Revelation condemns those who are neither for nor against as being lukewarm, and the Lord did not have very nice things to say about that.

Today, we are faced with a similar challenge, for there are reports of messages and visions seemingly coming from all over the world. How do we react to them? Do we dismiss them as pious talk, waiting for official approval before we accept them; or do we act on them? So living at the time of Jesus would not have made things any easier to accept.

When Jesus ascended into heaven he did not remove his presence from the earth; rather he made it possible for himself constantly to be present everywhere on the earth. Before his resurrection he was confined to the place where his body was. So, in order to hear him speak or have him lay his hands on us, we would have had to find out where he was, and even that was no guarantee that we would be able to get near him, for everyone was wanting to touch him. The chances of seeing him personally would have been practically nil.

Today, Jesus is present in his Church and we do not have to go very far to hear his word or receive his healing touch.

In the last chapter we saw what God was achieving through the death and resurrection of his Son. Jesus died for everyone, therefore his work of salvation must be made available to everyone. Salvation is much more than a passport to heaven; salvation includes being delivered from our self-centredness, being set free to live for others and for the welfare of all on earth. The Church continues this work of Jesus through the power of the Holy Spirit by teaching and ministering the sacraments.

I would be very reluctant to lay down hard and fast rules about how everyone can have the saving work of Jesus applied to them. It is certainly through the activity of the Holy Spirit that the saving work of Jesus is brought to individuals; but once we start judging who is saved and who isn't, then we get into trouble. God is the judge, not us. On the other hand it is for our comfort that we are able to know when God's saving work is affecting us.

Growth of the Church

It is important to understand that the Church has not always been as we see her today. It is strange how we can all but imagine Jesus in Mass vestments, or see the early Church clothed in our modern-day idea of Church. Jesus never told his disciples how to baptise nor how to say Mass. He just said, 'Go, baptise them in the name of the Father and of the Son and of the Holy Spirit' and at the Last Supper he commanded, 'Do this in memory of me'.

It was only gradually as the occasions began to arise that the apostles gathered to make decisions about what the Lord had taught them. Today, many taxing questions have arisen and the Church has to gather and make momentous decisions, interpreting the Lord's mind with the aid of the Holy Spirit. This is no easy task and it was the same for the early Church as it began to deal with problems and developments. One cannot find explicit teaching from the Lord on all seven sacraments, but clearly in interpreting the teaching of the Lord the early Church recognised certain moments when the Lord's saving work needed to be applied to an individual.

Sacraments are visible signs

Sacraments are external, visible signs indicating that the saving work of the Lord is being accomplished within us at that moment. They are for our comfort. We can trust that when certain signs are done, certain words said, and conditions met, then the saving work of Jesus for a specific purpose is applied at that moment.

It is important to know that God is not tied down to sacraments. He is the One who saves and he can dispense his saving grace when he wills and to whom he wills.

Jesus came to forgive sin and take it away

When Jesus began his mission of redemption, he came among a people who had been carefully schooled in the belief there was only one God, and he was Yahweh. He had the immensely difficult task of revealing that he was the Son of God and yet was not another God, and that he was the one who would remove sin by taking it upon himself. He had to unfold this ministry gradually.

The chosen people had a history of frequent lapses into idolatry, and when they were brought to repentance, the external form usually involved the sacrifice of a lamb. The shedding of the lamb's blood was seen as a life being offered in reparation for a life which had gone wrong.

Jesus began his mission with a call to repent and receive the good news of the forgiveness of sins. He then began to unpack who he was and why he had come. When Jesus claimed the power to forgive sins, he met head on the Jewish belief that only God could forgive sin. By demonstrating physical healings, which could be seen and verified, Jesus was leading them to believe that he also had power in the spiritual realm. When the paralytic was lowered through the roof, Jesus said to him: 'Courage, my child, your sins are forgiven' (Matt. 9:2).

The scribes reacted to this, claiming that only God could forgive sins. Jesus replied:

'Which of these is easier: to say, "Your sins are forgiven" or to say, "Get up and walk"? But to prove to you that the Son of man has authority on earth to forgive sins,' – he said to the paralytic

– 'get up, and pick up your bed and go off home'. And the man got up and went home. (9:5–8)

Jesus is the means of forgiveness

Later Jesus began to teach that he was to be the very means by which this forgiveness was to be obtained. 'The Son of Man came not to be served but to serve, and give his life as a ransom for many' (Matt. 20:28). That truth was again brought out at the Last Supper when he said: 'For this is my blood, the blood of the new covenant, shed for many for the forgiveness of sins.'

Jesus hands on the power to forgive

Jesus next began to teach that his disciples were also to hand on this reconciliation (2 Cor. 5:18). First of all he told Peter that what he bound on earth was also bound in heaven and what he loosed on earth was also loosed in heaven (Matt. 16:19). After his resurrection he breathed on his apostles saying: 'Receive the Holy Spirit. For those whose sins you forgive, they are forgiven; for those whose sins you retain, they are retained' (John 20:23).

The power to retain sins indicates that in some way the apostles had to hear what the sins were so that they could judge whether to forgive or retain. The power to forgive was not the power to forgive in their own name but the power to make effective the Lord's redemption in others. 'It is all God's work. It was God who reconciled us to himself through Christ and gave us the work of handing on this reconciliation' (2 Cor. 5:18).

Sins committed after baptism

Jesus never told his apostles exactly how they were to forgive sins, just as God never told Adam and Eve how they were to subdue the world. It seems as though at first the Apostles understood baptism as the way sins were to be forgiven, for the Lord did give them an explicit command to baptise for the forgiveness of sins. Being a Christian was costly, so the first converts were very zealous and devout. But gradually they had to face the problem of those who sinned seriously after their baptism. Matthew, in his Gospel, records Jesus' teaching on a brother who would not receive correction (18:15–18). Paul, in 1 Corinthians 5:1–13, addresses the problem of serious sexual sin and in the Acts of the Apostles we have the story of Ananias and his wife Sapphira deceiving the apostles – so clearly they were encountering the problem of sin after baptism.

We have no record of the sacrament of reconciliation operating until the third century. This does not mean it did not operate – we just have no record of it. It cannot have been easy for the early Church to begin to face the question of sins committed after baptism. Imagine yourself present at one of those meetings. Here we see the Church learning to be Church: learning to trust that it has received the Holy Spirit, but not imagining that this meant instant revelation, but that they needed to meet, pray, recall what the Lord taught and begin to make decisions. This was no easy task. We live at a time when we often imagine that either all the decisions have been made and all we have to do is to see what the Church did in earlier days, or we imagine that we are going to reach decisions by logic and reasoning alone.

Early ways of applying forgiveness

As the Church began to see it had a right to remit sins committed after baptism, this remission was, at first, for serious sins such as murder, apostasy, adultery and others. This remission, they felt, could only be granted once in a lifetime and it was even known as 'second baptism' or 'second penance'.

These sins were to be confessed to the bishop in secret, but the penance was to be performed publicly. Sinners were excluded from the Eucharist, thus demonstrating that sin cuts us off from God. Absolution for sins was not given until after the penance had been performed, for doing the penance was seen as a true sign of repentance. The penitents also had to wear special dress and only hear the Word liturgy at the Eucharist. Because of the practice of public penance this sacrament came to be known as the 'sacrament of penance'. Later, when the penance was no longer practised in public, it was known as 'confession'. As before, absolution for the sins was not given until after the penance had been performed, to ensure true repentance. This absolution was given on Maundy Thursday at a celebration known as 'sacramentum reconciliationis' and after this ceremony the sinners were allowed to take their place in the community again. It was from this ceremony that Vatican II derived the name 'sacrament of reconciliation'.

Changes over the centuries

Because the penances were so severe – strict fasting, the wearing of sackcloth and ashes, kneeling outside the church during services, banishment from taking part in church ceremonies – this sacrament was often postponed until the hour of death. In the fifth century Cassian refers to alternative forms of penance such as acts of charity, almsgiving, acceptance of sufferings, intercession.

It was from St Patrick and his monks that a new form for the sacrament began to appear. The penances were no longer performed in public, though they were still quite severe. More frequent confession was encouraged and to help this, the confession needed no longer be made to the bishop but to any priest. People were encouraged to include less serious sins in the confession, and in time this sacrament was no longer confined to dealing with serious sins. Again, the penances were still quite heavy, including serious fasting, long prayers and pilgrimages to Rome or the Holy Land, and alternative penances were sought. In the twelfth century Abelard attacked the external practice of penance and pointed out that the gospel called for repentance in the heart.

Vatican II changes

Pope John XXIII called for a second Vatican Council to complete the unfinished work of Vatican I, which had to close down because of the Franco-Prussian war. During the Vatican II Council, which undertook to update the Church, the sacrament of forgiveness underwent certain changes. Drawing on the vast information available and world-wide experience, the Church was anxious that this sacrament should find its rightful place in the modern Church. The name was changed from 'confession' to 'reconciliation' to emphasise that it was God's work 'reconciling the world to himself in Christ', whereas 'penance' or 'confession' put the stress on human action.

Also the Church wished that there should be a diversity of ways that the sacrament could be celebrated, and that communal celebration be added to the individual form. The Word of God was recommended, either to be read privately before meeting with the priest, or together with him in the confessional. This was to proclaim the mercy and forgiveness of God, inspiring confidence and hope in the heart of the sinner. Many other changes were suggested and we will be looking at these in a later chapter. But before we consider them we need to look again at God's way of dealing with sin and how forgiveness is brought to each individual.

Need for faith

Sacraments are not magic. We have the word of the Church that they work, whether we feel that they do or not. Sometimes people wonder after receiving a sacrament if it 'worked' for they felt nothing at the time. We must trust in the Church, which teaches that the saving work of Jesus is made applicable to us no matter what we may feel at the time. This does not mean that we just trust in the power of the sacraments and make no effort to prepare and receive them worthily. A row of communicants all receive the Lord, but the effect in each is different according to their disposition. Our eyes must not just be fixed on the sacrament, rather we must focus on the Lord who is touching us through this sacrament.

Faith must be added to sacraments. The sacraments are making effective in us what the Lord has already achieved, so it is very necessary to know what the Lord has achieved and to believe in it.

When Jesus was touched by the woman who had suffered from a haemorrhage for twelve years, she was healed. Many others were touching him at that moment too, but no power went out of him. The reason is that she had faith in him; but note, having faith in him was not enough, she also needed to touch him.

I like to see sacraments as when we approach the Lord and allow him to touch us through his Church. Just as the woman needed to have faith, so too we need to have faith in what the Lord has done for us and ask him to make it effective in us at this moment of touching.

Other ways of reconciliation

Reconciliation is not the only way sins can be remitted. They can be remitted through works of charity or by confessing directly to God. Whenever we acknowledge our sins to God, whether in the confessional or outside, Jesus turns to the Father and says: 'I have dealt with that.' The Spirit of God applies that forgiveness there and then.

If that is so, then why do we need this sacrament?

We need it, first of all, for serious sins, but it is also good to expose our other sins to the power of the sacrament. Also sin is not just between us and God, it is between us and the brothers and sisters in the Church, and God. Just as in the human body, when one member is damaged or has become sick, this will affect the whole body in some way, so also when we live a life of sin, we weaken the body of Christ present in this world and we weaken the spiritual life of the body. We need to ask pardon of the whole body for our offence. By going to the representative of the Church, we are confessing to the whole Church through that representative.

This, of course, does not excuse us from seeking pardon of individuals when we harm them by sin. If we should take away the good name of someone, we need to confess that to God, through the Church's representative, and we also need to make restitution to the individual we have offended and ask for forgiveness.

5

Exposing the Right Sins

 In the chapter after this one, we will look at the New Rite of Reconciliation step by step, trying to sense the thinking behind the changes, so as to use the sacrament more profitably. Before we do that, some time must be spent in trying to identify our sins and the sin that lies hidden within us. We have seen that sin dulls our spiritual perception, and this can make us very blind to our own sin.

As mentioned already, we did not become sinners the day we committed our first sin; we were born sinners. A sinner is not someone who just commits sins, it is someone in whom sin dwells. Long before sin becomes visible in some action, it is present within us – it is a flaw within, a disposition, a tendency, a proneness towards evil. Jesus did not just come to atone for our committed sins, he came to take away the sin lurking within us.

The blood of animals was incapable of taking sin away, but it was a good illustration that in some way a life had to be laid down in reparation for a life which had gone wrong. The blood of the Son of God was more than capable of atoning for sin; and through the offering of his sinless flesh, sinful flesh was renewed for all who put their faith in him.

In the sacrament of reconciliation two things happen. Our committed sins are forgiven, remitted; and our sin within us is put to death and our new life in Christ is strengthened.

Need to expose the right sins

If the sacrament of reconciliation is to have its two-fold effect, then we need to try and identify the sin within us from which our sinful actions come. Failing to see and confess the inward disposition means we will fail to apply God's remedy for our healing. What is so insidious about sin is that it injects dullness into us; it blinds us, blurs us spiritually, making us unaware of the true situation and because of this we fail to admit the sin so cleverly hidden in us.

What is the sin behind our sin?

If a healing ointment is to be effective, it needs to be applied to the wounded area. In the same way, if this sacrament is to have its healing effect, then we need to know where to let it beam its rays. Where possible we need to confess not just our sinful actions, but also the sinful dispositions that lie behind those acts.

For example, three penitents may all confess to having been unkind. In each case the three sins are very different, yet they are cloaked under the same heading 'being unkind'.

A priest is a shepherd: he is not just curious, he is a pastor and wishes his flock to grow to maturity and full spiritual strength. In asking how the sin of unkindness occurred, he is leading the penitent to better self-understanding. The first penitent has had one of those days when everything went wrong from the very moment she got out of bed. On her arrival home that night, after a very trying day, she found a friend on the doorstep wanting assistance. This was the straw that broke the camel's back, and she blew her stack.

Through talking things over, the priest was able to point out that maybe she was living her life reacting to it by what she felt and failing to remember the Lord's promise to be with her and share her life. The sin she needed to confess was her failure to remember the Lord's promises – a failure to live in that place of peace.

The second penitent was unkind because of jealousy. Someone where he worked was brighter and more efficient, and was also younger, so therefore was a threat to him, causing the penitent consistently to be unkind. Clearly this sin is more serious than that in the previous example because it was very deliberate and was not rising out of frustration or hot-headedness. So the sin that needed to be exposed to the power of the sacrament was jealousy.

The third penitent who confessed to being unkind was someone who was totally absorbed in herself. She felt she was the only pebble on the beach and so it is not surprising she was unkind in her dealings with others. The sin that needed confessing was that of over self-concern.

Sinful attitudes

All this helps us to see it is not only the sins we commit that need to be looked at but we also need to turn our attention to the sin within from where they come. This is not so easy to see and that is why talking things over with another can be very illuminating in uncovering the real sin.

The wound of the Fall manifests its presence in us in different ways. Some people have quick tempers; others are pushy and always trying to be in the centre of everything; others are lustful; others seem to have problems with honesty and are very weak when an opportunity comes to take something that is not theirs. How these faults get attached to different people, I do not know. Obviously life can give us raw deals, we can get hurt by living and we develop ways of coping. We are also born with different dispositions and these we can name 'original sin'.

In trying to be conscious of the sin within us, we do not want to become self-probing, doing endless dissections trying to discover our inner sin. We need to ask the Holy Spirit for his illumination, for Jesus told us the Spirit would convict us of sin.

Of course the evil spirit also wants to point out our sin, if he knows we are the type who will give in to guilty feelings and anxiety. When the Holy Spirit points out our sin, he comforts us by reminding us that there is a remedy for sin and that is in the Cross of Jesus Christ. So if, when we ask the

Spirit to show us our sins, we find that we become depressed, we should consider whether perhaps the other spirit is at work.

We saw earlier that sin is fundamentally a refusal to acknowledge God as God with absolute right over us. All sin asserts that we are our own master. We may be able to label our sins with names such as lust, jealousy, avarice or some such thing – they all, in fact, stem from the originating sin of rebellion which lies within us. We need to look and see how much of that rebellion is still within us. Just because we go to church, make efforts to practise our faith, we can tend to think of ourselves as good and loyal Christians, and never see the rebellion that is deep within us all. Clear rebellion is fairly obvious to see, but it is the secret rebellion that hides under the guise of religion which is the most subtle.

All sin, fundamentally, is us saying to God that we will go our way and not his. It is good to take an honest look at ourselves and ask, is God first in our lives? Some will be able to admit, straightaway, that he is not. But those who practise Christianity, go to church and endeavour to do what is right, will probably find difficulty in admitting that God may not be first in their life. There is no need to get full of guilt over this, we may well have to admit simply that it is true. It is sad, but it is true. What God wants is that we dare to admit it and ask him to heal us. We cannot ask for healing if we do not think we need it.

If we begin to see how wilful we are, and do not try and hide from that unpleasant truth, then there is a chance that God will begin to do in us what we are unable to do. Very rarely is unbelief confessed, yet it is the most common of sins. We tend to think of it as a sin that belongs to unbelievers. The truth is we just do not believe enough.

Sinful attitudes form us and shape us. For example a self-centred person, constantly putting self first, will meet every situation with the question: 'what is in it for me?' It will not be recognised as selfish. Such phrases from the gospel as 'Come to me all who are heavy burdened' or 'God is close to the broken-hearted' can all be heard willingly and gladly, not because we are God-centred, but because we are self-centred with a darkened mind.

In his teaching 'Blessed are the poor in spirit' (Matt. 5:3) Jesus is saying blessed are you when you discover your spiritual poverty. That discovery is a blessed moment for then the need for God is seen in all its starkness. Such a discovery is gall to self-love, and we can fail to face the hurt and disappointment, and instead immerse ourselves in external activity to prove our worth to ourselves and others.

Jesus came to rescue us from such cloying experiences and often we cannot discover these things by ourselves.

6

The New Rite

 Since Vatican II the Church has encouraged a more mature use of the sacrament. For some it had become a bit like a laundromat – you put your list of sins in and out came your absolution. By recommending a room instead of a confessional box, a room where either a face to face meeting or anonymity can be offered, much of the forbidding atmosphere of the dark box has been dispelled. Many have awful memories of this stemming from childhood days, some even have phobias as a result.

The Church also wants to get away from lists of sins and would prefer we dialogued more with the priest. This opportunity to chat with a priest can lead us to a greater self-understanding, bringing us to deeper insights as to where our real sin lies.

So we are encouraged to be less formal or stereotyped in the way we confess, but it is proving quite difficult to break out of the formal ways we have learnt. Confessing our sins is not something we do easily, and it did help a lot to have a set pattern to follow. We asked for a blessing, said how long it was since our last confession, told our sins, received a penance, made our act of contrition, received absolution and left. There was nothing wrong with this, save that it could so easily become a formula with little meaning.

Whenever we go to receive any sacrament we need to remind ourselves of what we are actually about. It is so easy just to 'go to the sacraments'. In the sacrament of reconciliation, we are, in a sense, collecting what Jesus has won for us on Calvary with such terrible cost. Therefore, if we are going to draw the most benefit from this, we need to prepare ourselves.

Let me give an example of how stereotyped we have become. I have often found that, after a chat with someone during which sins have actually been confessed, when I have suggested that they might like to receive absolution, the person has then adopted a strange stance, made the sign of the cross and said: 'Oh bless me, father, for I have sinned' and proceeded to say how long it has been since their last confession. In other words they became quite unnatural. When I pointed out that they had actually already confessed their sins and there was no need to repeat them, they seemed to relax and become normal again.

Preparation

The Church encourages us to read passages from Scripture, especially passages concerned with heal-ing or forgiveness. This is to stir up our faith and trust in God's love. If Jesus, before his death and resurrection, forgave sins and healed people, what can he not do now that he is risen?

Faith is not something we either have or do not have, like beans in a jar; faith is something that must be used, it must be kept active. To believe what Jesus has done, we need to stir up in ourselves confidence that he also came to heal us. Knowing that Jesus came for sinners, gives us fresh heart; therefore reading passages of Scripture which tell about Jesus' love for sinners (Mark 2:15–17; Luke 15:1; Luke 15:11–32) helps us to approach this sacrament with confidence in spite of our sins.

Examen

Remembering what we saw in the last chapter about how sin blinds us and makes us insensitive to its evil, we need to ask the Holy Spirit to enlighten our minds and show us our real sins. If we are not in the habit of reviewing our day each evening, nor in the habit of frequent confession, then this becomes more difficult and it is easy to fall back on lists and numbers.

Admitting our sins and failures is never easy, and people often put little prefixes to their sins. They will say: 'Maybe I have been a little unkind. Maybe I have not lived up to my Christian calling.' All this is understandable, but in fact it is failing to confess honestly. The truth is you either have done these things or you have not. We need to be simple and state what happened. There is no necessity to go into endless details. The honesty of some is most moving.

There are pamphlets or small books that help us

examine our lives. Many find these helpful. I personally find that I can say yes to nearly all the suggestions, and things then get a bit unwieldy.

We all have some sin which is our particular weakness. If we do not know that, then we need to ask the Holy Spirit to show us. Once we know it, we need to look and see why we often fall into that sin. Remember the examples we looked at where unkindness was cloaking several different sins.

While many confessions are edifying, many are woefully unprepared. It can be quite depressing trying to help people look deeper into their lives; you end up wondering if they have any clue as to what it is all about. This is why I have become so convinced about sin blinding us. I have experienced this blindness myself and while most people are not culpable, it is distressing to see how much ignorance exists as to what the gospel is about.

How to begin

The usual way to start is to ask for a blessing, unless the priest has already given one, and then say how long it is since the last confession. This helps the priest for if there are long gaps between each occasion, he may see the wisdom of suggesting a more frequent use of the sacrament. I remember hearing confessions in the West Indies, where I was recuperating after sickness. One small lad started his confession with: 'Bless me, father, for I have sinned. This is my last confession.' I resisted telling him to make sure it was a good one.

The confession of sins

We have spent some time trying to see our real sins, but are any of us able to express those sins in adequate words? Are any of us able to be that honest? I do not think we need to get over-worried about this. I like to think that the words of Jesus, 'Father, forgive them; they know not what they do', are repeated again as we stumble along trying in all honesty to speak in very broken phrases of our sins. Again and again I ponder the saying of St Paul: 'God made the sinless one into sin'. Has Jesus so taken on our sins that in a sense he has already confessed them to the Father? Such a thought as that makes me see the value of confessing to a priest and not just privately to God. When we participate in the sacraments, we are no longer just an individual, we are members of the body of Christ and our actions become his. I remember being taught something about how our imperfect sorrow was made perfect sorrow in this sacrament. For a long time I never really grasped what that meant, but now I think I do see. When we confess directly to God, it is us confessing, but when we confess in the sacrament, then Jesus confesses with us, in us and through us.

What helps me is to know that as I say my sins, Jesus in some way is claiming my sins and telling the Father that he has already dealt with them.

Advice

After we have confessed our sins the priest may want to give some advice or encouragement. At these moments the Holy Spirit can operate in a remarkable way, inspiring the priest to say the right thing, or ask the correct question. Remember, the priest himself has to go to confession and as a penitent-priest he has to admit his sins and failures.

Penance

Normally then the priest gives a penance. We must be clear that it is *not* the performing of the penance that wins the forgiveness of our sins. Our sins have already been forgiven through the death of the Lord, and all we are doing at confession is collecting that forgiveness. As we mention our sins, it is as though Jesus is turning to his Father and saying that he has already dealt with those sins, and he then sends the Holy Spirit to us to apply that forgiveness. If this is so, then why do we get a penance? In the old days one was required to do the penance before one received the absolution. It was a sign of repentance and a mark of a change of heart. Now we receive absolution before we perform the penance. Performing our penance is a sign of our desire to change our ways.

The penance also has something to do with reparation. When someone confesses to stealing, then forgiveness cannot be granted unless the thing stolen is returned. This does not have to be done publicly and if it is impossible to return what was stolen, then some reparation has to be made. When we sin, several people get hurt: firstly God, secondly the Body of Christ, either directly or indirectly, thirdly ourselves. In the sacrament our relationship with God is restored, but the damage we may have caused another is not repaired, nor is the damage done to myself. For example, if I have told lies, I get into the habit of doing that; in confessing the sin, I get pardon but not deliverance from the habit.

I feel there is still work to be done in this area, for the giving of three Hail Marys, or some such penance, often bears no resemblance to the damage caused by our sins. Obviously if unkindness has been confessed, then some sort of reconciliation is suitable. When something has been stolen then restitution has to be made. I feel, where possible, the penance ought to bear some relationship to the confession. On the few occasions when I have tried to be more creative and have given some suitable penance, the penitent has often said at the end of the interview: 'You never gave me a penance, father!'

Act of contrition

There are many forms of acts of contrition, some of which are not ideal for today. I think we need to study the act that we use and see if it really is saying what we would like to say. Many people now make their own acts of sorrow, and these can be very moving.

Absolution

While the priest is giving us the absolution we should listen carefully to the words and deliberately receive them. Now that it is in English and not in Latin, there is no need to make our act of contrition while the priest is saying the absolution. The words sum up most suitably what is actually happening. In a few lines the mystery of Christ's saving death is stated. We need to listen carefully, saying to ourselves, 'So let it be, amen, amen'.

The priest begins the absolution with the beautiful words: 'God, the Father of mercies'. He does not say 'Merciful Father', but the 'Father of mercies'. Then he goes on to state the truth: 'God, the Father of mercies, through the death and resurrection of his Son, has reconciled this world to himself and sent the Holy Spirit among us for the forgiveness of sins'. What sparcity of words and yet how they capture the basic truth. Jesus' death has reconciled us to the Father and the Holy Spirit is now being sent upon the penitent to apply that forgiveness. The priest goes on: 'through the ministry of the Church' – this means you have the guarantee of the whole Church behind this – 'may God give you pardon and peace, and I absolve you from your sins in the name of the Father, and of the Son, and of the Holy Spirit. Amen.' Notice the priest does not say, 'I forgive you your sins', he says, 'I absolve you', that means 'I free you, I loose you from, I break you free'. He often ends by saying, 'Go now, your sins are forgiven.'

I would like to invent a confessional where the priest presses a button at the end of the absolution and trumpets blow. Something stupendous has happened; yet if you stand outside the box and look at the people coming out, you would not imagine that any sin had been forgiven. We need to exercise our faith on what has happened. Too often we judge by our feelings – and that is not the way a Christian should live.

Frequency

It is sad that this sacrament, which was once often practised, has fallen into very rare use by many now. We were encouraged to go frequently and that, under the old understanding of the sacrament, was not wrong. In trying to get a more mature approach, frequency has not been stressed, and there has been more emphasis on the quality of the confession, with the expectation that people would go to confession less often. We are creatures of habit and, if we were once in the habit of going every week or two, it seems much harder to be regular when the period in between is longer. I would not like to regulate just how often a person ought to go, but clearly if the gap between confessions is quite long, then the ability to see accurately what our real sins are will be greatly reduced. People who leave several months between confessions, seem to have difficulty in remembering their sins, and they tend to resort to 'five lies, four impure thoughts, and twenty-seven swear words'. There is little evidence that much thought has gone into such a confession and one wonders how genuine the repentance is.

It takes time for us to change our ways and become familiar with new ones. Confessing our sins is never easy, and finding someone with whom we feel at home, even when face to face, can be a problem. But, remember priests also go to confession, and they also feel the difficulty. But if we keep our eyes on what is actually happening at confession, remembering that what took place with such cost on Calvary is now being applied to us, I think we can learn to cope with the embarrassment.

7

You Have Set Us Free

Jesus came to free us from sin, not just to forgive our sins. He died to pay for our sins and he rose to new life so that we, sharing in that new life, might live free from slavery to sin.

When a priest absolves he does not say, 'I forgive you your sins', but rather, 'I absolve you from your sins'. Absolving is more than forgiveness, it means breaking free from, a loosening of chains, a healing.

This breaking free, this loosening from sin, is not experienced by many. If anything, the opposite seems to be the norm: sin remains and does not go away. Why is this so? If Satan has been defeated by the Lord through the Cross and resurrection, how is it he still seems to roam about this planet with so much power?

I believe the reason for this is because clear teaching is not given. It is not easy to accept that we are dead in Christ to sin, because we seem anything but dead. Things that are hard to teach often get neglected, and what is not taught does not have faith put in it. To experience the power of Christ's victory, we need to know what that victory is so that we can put our faith in it – for we cannot put our faith in what we do not know.

What is this victory?

The victory – the central theme of the gospel – is that Christ snatched us out of Satan's hands by dying for our sins *and* rose again that we might live in a new way.

We need to unwrap this truth. The laying down of human life that took place on Calvary was more than enough to outweigh all human sins, because that life belonged to the second person of the Trinity. This was God's marvellous plan: human sins should be atoned for by one of the human family who would be capable of obtaining such forgiveness because he was also God. This is celebrated in the Preface III for Sundays in ordinary time: 'You came to our rescue by your power as God, but you wanted us to be saved by one like us.'

But that is not all. Because Jesus is our representative, when he died, all whom he represented also died. We did not die in ourselves, we died *in him*. This is the important truth – *we died in him*.

In order that this death might become a reality in us, we need to accept Christ as our representative. The way we do so is by being baptised into him. We have all been taught that at baptism we were baptised into Christ's death and rose with him that we might live with him in a new way (see Rom. 6:3,4). This truth was demonstrated in the old ritual of baptism when total immersion was practised. The going down into the water represented our dying and descending into the tomb; the rising up represented our being born again into a new life in Christ.

This dying at baptism takes place in the realm of the spirit, not in the realm of the senses or of reason. We have but the first fruits of salvation (Rom. 8:22–4). What takes place in the spirit cannot be felt by the senses, nor really grasped by reason. It is not contrary to reason, just beyond it. It is in this state that we must acknowledge that we live.

The deceiver is still at work

If this doctrine is the very heart of the gospel, then we can be sure that Satan, the father of lies, will do all in his considerable power to obscure it and prevent it from being known. For a very long time I saw the gospel in moralistic terms – be good and you will merit heaven – and I do not believe that I had such a misconception purely by chance. I hadn't really grasped at all that salvation is a *gift* from God the Father through Christ Jesus his Son.

In his general audience on 15 November 1972, Pope Paul VI asked the question, 'What is the greatest need of the Church?' This is how he replied: 'Do not let our answer surprise you as being over simple or even superstitious and unreal: one of the greatest needs is defence from that evil which is called the Devil. Evil is not merely a lack of something, but an effective agent, a living spiritual being, perverted and perverting.'

Knowing a doctrine is not the same as believing in it. If Satan cannot prevent us from hearing the truth, then he is quite content if we let it lie fallow.

We are not dealing in magic here. It is not enough to know the Lord is the Saviour and just to call on his saving power. It is our *faith in* the Lord's saving that releases that power. It is one thing to have been taught that the Lord's death and resurrection saves us, it is quite something else to believe in it and act on it.

God always requires our co-operation with him. He pays us an immense compliment by asking us to work with him. For example, when Christ cured the paralytic, he told him to 'get up and walk'. The Lord did not do that for him; he cured him, and then told him to act on that cure. Again when he sent his apostles out to preach the gospel and heal the sick, they had to obey his word and act on his command. So we, also, have to obey what we hear. Our sins have not only been forgiven, their hold on us has been broken – we have been absolved. We must act on that.

What about will-power?

Often I have asked penitents, after they have confessed their sins, how they plan not to commit those sins again, and I have rarely been given the right answer. The answer usually is, 'I'll try harder, father', and this shows that the penitent still imagines that will-power can conquer sin.

It is not that will-power is not required; the will, however, does not need to determine to make every effort to overcome the fault, but rather to accept God's way of overcoming sin, which is through the death and resurrection of Jesus Christ. 'Lord, by your Cross and resurrection, you have set us free', as we say at Mass. If we are consistently neglecting to use what we say with our lips, then it is not surprising that we do not experience the gospel as power. St Paul tells us, 'I am not ashamed of the Good News: it is the power of God saving all those who have faith' (Rom. 1:16). Satan can make us misunderstand those words and cause us to focus our mind on 'all those who have faith', comforting us that we have faith because we are Catholics. Being in the Church is no guarantee that we believe in the heart of the gospel. We will only experience the power of the gospel when we passionately believe in the death and resurrection of the Lord. Notice, I did not say that we believe *that* it took place; rather we believe in what happened *because* it took place.

Some penitents answer the question, 'How do you plan not to commit those sins again?' by saying that they will pray. Now, while prayer is essential, it all depends on what is meant by prayer. To pray, begging God to set us free, is surely a good thing. It seems so right and correct. But that sort of prayer actually bypasses the essential truth of the gospel – the truth that God *has already acted for our deliverance*.

Ignorance

I fear that much of today's spirituality neglects this central truth and the very heart of the gospel gets left out. I can well remember thinking the gospel was all about being good and trying desperately to practise what Jesus taught. Naturally I prayed for strength to be patient, generous, pure. What is so deceptive is that it all seems right and proper. But to pray to God, as though it was up to us by our prayers to persuade him to act and do something to deliver us, when all the time he has already acted and done everything that is necessary, seems to me to be a gross neglect of an essential truth. We all agree that prayer is a good and a necessary thing, but when we are led to bypass the central truth of the gospel, I fear we have been greatly deceived.

We need to proclaim the truth that Jesus has over-come, and we need to come against all opposition using that truth. This is not magic, nor does it mean that God will do our will, but it does mean that we ask God to act using what his Son has already achieved.

Our task is to learn to live in Christ. Our constant temptation is to act outside Christ. Deep down in us is the drive to act on our own. We are *in Christ*, but if we act as though we were not in him, then we effectively act outside Christ. That is why Jesus said, 'Abide in me' (John 15:4).

Coping with temptation

Temptation, of course, will still attack us for we are not yet fully redeemed. When we sin we step out from the shelter where Christ has put us, exposing ourselves to evil. Temptation is to be dealt with, not by trying to resist with our own strength, but by putting it to death with the truth that, in Christ, we are dead to sin (as St Paul says in Romans 6). But what does it mean to be 'dead to sin'? I remember wrestling with this statement when I first began to pay attention to Romans 6. I would argue that I was not 'dead to sin' because I *did* sin. I began to realise that I did not actually believe this doctrine and so it was not surprising that I did not experience its effect in my life. It helped when someone told me that Scripture did not say that sin was dead to me, but that I, in Christ, was dead to sin. I started to see that I was being tempted to deny that I was in Christ and to follow the demands of temptation which I could feel very strongly.

Paul writes in Colossians, 'You must kill everything in you that belongs only to earthly life' (3:5). In another place he says, 'You cannot belong to Christ Jesus unless you crucify all self-indulgent passions and desires' (Gal. 5:24).

In practical terms this means learning to live in the fact that we are dead to sin in Christ, and when Satan attacks us, we retaliate with the truth that we are dead to this way of living and thus crucify the desires that are seeking our attention.

What we need to understand is that sacraments endure; they are not confined to the ceremony where they are administered. At baptism we both died and rose to new life in Christ and we are to live this truth throughout the whole of our lives. We must die to self every moment and rise to new life in Christ. To apply this truth to every rebellious thought is to put that thought to death with the truth.

When temptation attacks, our action must not be to try and resist in our own power, but to defend ourselves with the truth: 'I have died with Christ to that way of living. I have been bought with a great price and therefore I no longer have to submit as your slave. I belong to the Lord Jesus Christ.' Of course we do not use these exact words; to do so could verge on treating them as magic. It is our faith in what the Lord has done that saves us; how we express that faith does not matter.

Praying through the gospel message

We have seen that arriving at this place of conviction is not achieved by filling our heads with teaching and Scripture quotes as if they provide some sort of magic formula. That would be another subtle way of self-achieving. Only the Holy Spirit can lead us on to truth. He has to bring us to that place where we see and admit our inability.

This place cannot be reached by reasoning, study, will-power or asceticism. It comes to those who wait, to those who give time to prayer, who no longer wrestle to master everything; it comes to those who are content to live with mystery. Prayer, in its earlier stages, involves thinking – we wrestle with thoughts and questions. But later, as we begin to realise that no amount of thinking or reasoning can reach or capture God, we begin to let our heart be involved. I do not mean we sit still and just wait trying to think of nothing. That is not possible, and it could result in a very passive waiting.

I hesitate to say what I try to do when I pray for fear someone should think that they ought to do the same. We all pray in our own unique way and we should pray in the way we *can* pray and not in the way we cannot. I, myself, tend to think of Christ, either on the Cross or just risen from the tomb, but I try not to reason it all out. I resist asking questions about how it all happened, why it all happened – I just accept it as a fact. Then I endeavour to respond with gratitude, wonder and worship. This could take the form of words of thanksgiving or gratitude or just thoughts. I suppose I could call it a moment of adoration or worship. It is at such moments that I can get insights, or understandings, which are not like understandings that come after reasoning processes. It does not always happen at the time of prayer, sometimes it comes at odd moments when I am busy somewhere else. It is a gift and there seems to be a *knowing* without knowing how or why. I believe this is what revelation means.

The journey out of self into God is of necessity slow. We have to learn to get out of the driving seat and allow God to be the Lord and Master. That is not quickly learnt. There is no crash course. It comes to those who ask and wait. God has to get us to that place where we know for certain that we cannot live this life by our own decisions. This is not an easy journey, and Satan has a field-day taking truths and twisting them so that they seem ridiculous to us. For example: to be told that nothing we can do will achieve freedom from sin, makes us think that therefore we have nothing to do at all. That is not true. It is like growing seeds; we do not make the seeds grow, but if we do not sow and water them they will not grow. On the other hand to be told that we have something to do, can make us think we have everything to do.

Where is this teaching in Scripture and liturgy?

I suppose it is all too easy to imagine that because a person goes to church, has perhaps attended a

Catholic school, he or she has a clear grasp of the central teaching of the gospel. It is, however, quite wrong to assume this. Careful teaching is needed all our lives, for while we might have learnt much Catholic doctrine, we can be very ignorant about the essential truth of Christianity.

The teaching about being dead to sin in Christ is not at all easy to grasp and like so many difficult doctrines it can get left aside. I do not remember having any clear teaching on the subject, but that does not mean I received none. When something does not catch your interest or understanding, you often do not take it in even when it is mentioned.

After I had become aware of the teaching and began to see its importance, I noticed that the liturgy constantly referred to it. I am amazed how, in spite of this frequent reference, I had never before really noticed it. This shows how important teaching is, for if we have not firmly grasped that truth, it will be missed. How many times did I say the prayer at the end of the rosary, and never take in what I was really saying?

O God, who through the life, death and resurrection of your Son, has purchased for us the rewards of eternal salvation . . .

It states clearly here that salvation comes through the death and resurrection of Christ. The following texts all refer to this truth, although it has to be said that they do it rather obliquely, so it can easily be missed.

He is the Word through whom you made the

universe, the Saviour you sent to redeem us. (Euch. II Preface)

All life, all holiness comes from You through your Son, Jesus Christ, by the working of the Holy Spirit. (Euch. III)

. . . see the victim whose death has reconciled us to yourself. (Euch. III)

We offer you his body and blood, the acceptable sacrifice which brings salvation to the whole world. (Euch. IV)

Father in heaven, the love of your Son led him to accept the suffering of the Cross, that we might glory in new life. (Prayer for fifth Sunday of Lent)

Lord God, the Cross reveals the mystery of your love: a stumbling block indeed for unbelief, but the sign of your power and wisdom to us who believe. Teach us to contemplate your Son's glorious Passion that we may always believe and glory in his Cross. (Evening prayer, Wednesday, second week)

We have numerous teachings of Scripture that are saying the same truth, but in the past we Catholics have not been so good at reading our Scripture. Today things are greatly changed, and we can be much more aware of texts like:

For anyone who is in Christ, there is a new creation; the old creation has gone, and now the new one is here. It is all God's work. (2 Cor. 5:17–18)

We must realise that our former selves have been crucified with him to destroy this sinful body and to free us from the slavery of sin. (Rom. 6:6).

77

Paul goes on:

> When Christ died, he died, once for all, to sin,
> so his life now is life with God; and in that way,
> you too must consider yourselves to be dead to
> sin but alive for God in Christ Jesus. (6:10,11)

Here we are given instructions on how to deal with
the sin within us. We are to consider ourselves dead
to sin but alive *in* Christ Jesus. We are to fight using
this truth, and yet so few have been taught it. When
the gospel is not experienced as power, then it
becomes irrelevant and loses its bite.

We will not feel this new creation for we have
but the first fruits of it. Salvation has not yet been
completed in us, but it has begun because we are
one with Christ in our spirit. Life's journey consists
of allowing this new life to penetrate into our whole
being.

If you put a brick into water, you can say, 'the
brick is in the water', but is the water in the brick?
In time, because bricks are usually porous, the water
will seep in. At baptism, we were put into Christ,
and our journey through life consists in allowing
Christ to enter into the whole of us.

We need to pray for revelation so that we might
be given insight into this mystery of our life in
Christ. No human knowledge can achieve it – it
comes only to those who humbly seek it from God.

St Bonaventure clearly speaks of this truth in a
treatise 'On the Mind's Journey to God'. He says,

> We must set aside all discursive operations of the
> intellect and turn the very apex of our soul to God

to be entirely transformed in him. This is most mystical and secret. No one knows it but he who receives it. No one receives it but he who desires it. No one desires it but he who is deeply penetrated by the fire of the Holy Spirit, the fire Christ sent on earth. This is why the apostle says that this mystical wisdom is revealed through the Holy Spirit. If you want to understand how this happens, ask it of grace, not of learning; ask it of desire, not of understanding; ask it of earnest prayer not attentive reading; ask it of the betrothed, not of the teachers; ask it of God, not man; ask it of darkness, not radiance. (Reading from Feast of St Bonaventure)

8

Reconciliation Services

 As we have seen, Christ came preaching repentance and good news. He made peace by shedding his blood on the Cross, and he empowered his Church to minister that reconciliation continually throughout the ages.

We have seen how the early church progressed from thinking of baptism as the only sacrament that took sins away, to seeing the necessity for an ongoing sacrament.

Jesus empowered his apostles to forgive sins and they in turn empowered their successors to continue this work. The Church is Christ's continuing presence among us, even though it is made up of fallible humans. Together we form the Body of Christ.

When anyone commits a sin, not only is God offended but the Church is also offended because its presence and power in the world is made less effective. Therefore reconciliation is not to be sought only from God, but also from the Body of Christ here on earth. A priest represents the Church and when we confess to him we are confessing both to God and to the Body of Christ.

The Second Vatican Council decreed, 'The rite and formulas of penance are to be revived in such a way that they more clearly express the nature and effects of this sacrament.' From this decree came the New Rite. The Council also drew up a rite whereby several penitents can be reconciled, thus emphasising the communal aspect of the sacrament.

Of its nature this sacrament is private and the Church wishes to retain that aspect, and yet it also wishes to bring out the fact that we are all sinners and we all need to forgive each other. The new rite for public penance services guards the confidential aspect in that sins are confessed privately to a priest, and brings out the communal side by means of a penitential service held in common.

In such services prayers are said, and Scripture is read, since it is good for people to hear those texts that show the Lord's mercy and forgiveness. A homily is given and again this offers an opportunity for the love and mercy of God to be emphasised. To help people to prepare for the sacrament, the leader suggests areas of sin to be looked at and motives to be examined. This also affords a good opportunity for us to consider our joint responsibility for conditions in the world. A carefully prepared service can help people exercise a more mature examination of their lives. Also this sort of service can help a congregation get ready for the various Church festivals, thus enabling the group as a whole to participate in the feasts with a sense of having prepared together.

I have been at services where the priests are not

closed away but sit in a place where they can be seen. Seeing others at confession and receiving absolution can help us understand that we are all sinners and we all need this healing.

Permission whereby general absolution could be given was also granted at Vatican II, but since then it has been decided that it is up to the local bishop to grant such permission. Where this is not allowed, services have been devised to retain the confessing of sins to a priest, but the absolution is delayed until the end and is then given to all those who have confessed. This is another way of emphasising a sense of community.

Dealing with large congregations at these penitential services is not all that easy. A good number of priests is required, otherwise it takes a long time for confessions to be heard. Alas, these days it is not always easy to gather a good number of priests, especially in more rural areas. When there are few priests, it can become tedious for those who confessed early on and for those still waiting their turn. It is difficult to know how to occupy those not actually involved in making their confession to a priest.

The new rite has also provided for a celebration without absolution. This sort of service can be useful for often we need time to examine our lives, and it is only over a period of time that we begin to see what is happening to us. Ash Wednesday can be a suitable opportunity for such a service, for it sets the mood for Lent and begins a preparation for a deeper kind of confession.

As I have already mentioned, Vatican I (1869–70) had to be ended prematurely when it had only had time to deal with four of the fifteen points on its agenda. Those four points all had to do with the head of the Church. It is not surprising that the period after that Council was focused on Rome and Church leaders. Pope John XXIII saw that Vatican I had not been finished so he called another Council to complete it. That is why it was called Vatican II. In that Council the body of the Church was discussed. Since then the Church has been trying to make us all more aware of the fact that we are a body and our lives are not just our private affair.

The changes which have taken place are not just an updating. There was and is still a real need to make sure the central message of the gospel is clear. All changes are for this end. Teaching is very important and we live at a time when we could so easily try and be accommodating to everyone that we fail to teach the essentials to our children.

God has done wonderful things for us through his Son Jesus Christ. The Church exists to teach what he has done and to minister to its children his healing which he bought for us at such terrible cost.

Further copies of Fr. Ian's books

God is Not Angry and Your Sins are Forgiven
The God Who Speaks and You Will Receive Power
This is My Body and How Can I Pray ?

*are available by mail order
from*

Goodnews Books & Audio

Tel: 01582 571011
Fax: 01582 571012
email: orders@goodnewsbooks.net
www.goodnewsbooks.net

Send for a Catalogue of Christian Books